Last of the Black Titans

This book series is dedicated to the radical love and actions of Paulo Freire, Jesus "Pato" Gomez, and Joe L. Kincheloe.

TRANSGRESSIONS: CULTURAL STUDIES AND EDUCATION

Cultural studies provides an analytical toolbox for both making sense of educational practice and extending the insights of educational professionals into their labors. In this context *Transgressions: Cultural Studies and Education* provides a collection of books in the domain that specify this assertion. Crafted for an audience of teachers, teacher educators, scholars and students of cultural studies and others interested in cultural studies and pedagogy, the series documents both the possibilities of and the controversies surrounding the intersection of cultural studies and education. The editors and the authors of this series do not assume that the interaction of cultural studies and education devalues other types of knowledge and analytical forms. Rather the intersection of these knowledge disciplines offers a rejuvenating, optimistic, and positive perspective on education and educational institutions. Some might describe its contribution as democratic, emancipatory, and transformative. The editors and authors maintain that cultural studies helps free educators from sterile, monolithic analyses that have for too long undermined efforts to think of educational practices by providing other words, new languages, and fresh metaphors. Operating in an interdisciplinary cosmos, *Transgressions: Cultural Studies and Education* is dedicated to exploring the ways cultural studies enhances the study and practice of education. With this in mind the series focuses in a non-exclusive way on popular culture as well as other dimensions of cultural studies including social theory, social justice and positionality, cultural dimensions of technological innovation, new media and media literacy, new forms of oppression emerging in an electronic hyperreality, and postcolonial global concerns. With these concerns in mind cultural studies scholars often argue that the realm of popular culture is the most powerful educational force in contemporary culture. Indeed, in the twenty-first century this pedagogical dynamic is sweeping through the entire world. Educators, they believe, must understand these emerging realities in order to gain an important voice in the pedagogical conversation.

Without an understanding of cultural pedagogy's (education that takes place outside of formal schooling) role in the shaping of individual identity – youth identity in particular – the role educators play in the lives of their students will continue to fade. Why do so many of our students feel that life is incomprehensible and devoid of meaning? What does it mean, teachers wonder, when young people are unable to describe their moods, their affective affiliation to the society around them. Meanings provided young people by mainstream institutions often do little to help them deal with their affective complexity, their difficulty negotiating the rift between meaning and affect. School knowledge and educational expectations seem as anachronistic as a ditto machine, not that learning ways of rational thought and making sense of the world are unimportant.

But school knowledge and educational expectations often have little to offer students about making sense of the way they feel, the way their affective lives are shaped. In no way do we argue that analysis of the production of youth in an electronic mediated world demands some "touchy-feely" educational superficiality. What is needed in this context is a rigorous analysis of the interrelationship between pedagogy, popular culture, meaning making, and youth subjectivity. In an era marked by youth depression, violence, and suicide such insights become extremely important, even life saving. Pessimism about the future is the common sense of many contemporary youth with its concomitant feeling that no one can make a difference.

If affective production can be shaped to reflect these perspectives, then it can be reshaped to lay the groundwork for optimism, passionate commitment, and transformative educational and political activity. In these ways cultural studies adds a dimension to the work of education unfilled by any other sub-discipline. This is what *Transgressions: Cultural Studies and Education* seeks to produce – literature on these issues that makes a difference. It seeks to publish studies that help those who work with young people, those individuals involved in the disciplines that study children and youth, and young people themselves improve their lives in these bizarre times.

Last of the Black Titans

The Role of Historically Black Colleges and Universities in the 21st Century

Greg Wiggan
University of North Carolina at Charlotte, USA

with Lakia Scott
Baylor University, USA

SENSE PUBLISHERS
ROTTERDAM/BOSTON/TAIPEI

A C.I.P. record for this book is available from the Library of Congress.

ISBN: 978-94-6300-320-9 (paperback)
ISBN: 978-94-6300-321-6 (hardback)
ISBN: 978-94-6300-322-3 (e-book)

Published by: Sense Publishers,
P.O. Box 21858,
3001 AW Rotterdam,
The Netherlands
https://www.sensepublishers.com/

Printed on acid-free paper

TABLE OF CONTENTS

ACKNOWLEDGEMENTS

I wish to thank my very first teacher, Mrs. Lyons, the renowned educator in Sav-la-Mar, Westmoreland, Jamaica, and my last teacher, Dr. Asa Hilliard. I owe my deepest gratitude to these two educators who have had a profound impact on my growth and development. I also wish to thank my mother and father (and Baba Hilliard and Brother Robby), who taught me to be firm even when faced by institutional racism and prejudice. And to the 'Vicker,' elder ancestor Errol Peynado, and the queen mothers, Mama Scott and Mama "P," and to the late, Mr. Clinton Scarlett, who was the top librarian in Sav-la-Mar for at least three decades, blessed love. To Queen Makeda and Empress Izana, blessed love. "In loving memory of Dr. John Henrik Clarke." – Greg Wiggan. "To Dr. Clarke, Dr. Ben, and Dr. Hilliard"

I would like to recognize members of my family. To my husband and best friend, Chadwick Scott, I need to thank you immensely for allowing me to follow this dream. As we welcome Chadley into this world, I need to also thank my parents, Paul and Collette Jones, for their unwavering support and understanding of my academic pursuits. And I would like to especially thank Dr. Wiggan for all of his help and support. – Lakia Scott

INTRODUCTION

Education under Siege, Last of the Black Titans

Historically Black Colleges and Universities (HBCUs) have—and continue to play a key role in the education of African Americans. In 1900, approximately 2,600 African Americans had postsecondary credentials, largely due to the efforts of public and private HBCUs (Jackson, 2001). One-hundred-and-ten years later, in the 2010–2011 academic year, the National Center for Education Statistics (NCES, 2013) reported that approximately 33,000 bachelor's degrees were conferred by HBCUs. In 2010, there were an estimated 4.6 million African Americans who had a college degree (JBHE, 2015). And in 2011, approximately 324,000 students were enrolled in the 100 HBCUs across the U.S. (NCES, 2013). HBCUs account for between 9% and 10% of African American undergraduate student enrollment (NCES, 2013; Thurgood Marshall Fund, 2015), and they continue to represent a great legacy in the history of Black higher education.

Founded in 1837 through a generous donation by Richard Humphreys, who was a Quaker and philanthropist, the Institute for Colored Youth in Pennsylvania (later called Cheyney University), was the first HBCU in America (Cheyney University, 2015). This institution was monumental in the formation of Black higher education. Since that time, many historical and contemporary figures began their trek in post-secondary education at HBCUs. William Edward Burghardt Du Bois [W.E.B. Du Bois], sociologist, historian, Pan-Africanist and Civil Rights activist, was an HBCU alumnus. Du Bois graduated from Fisk University [Nashville, Tennessee] in 1888. He continued his education and received a second Bachelor's degree in History, graduate degree in Sociology, and Ph.D. in History from Harvard University in 1895 (Harvard University Press, n.d.), the year he became the first African American to receive a doctorate degree from the institution. Much of Du Bois' work examined the race, class, economics and political struggles of African Americans, issues he first became conscious of while studying at Fisk University. His collection of essays, books, and other writings are seminal works and invaluable contributions to our understanding of race relations.

Similarly, Langston Hughes, renowned poet, playwright and social activist, also graduated from an HBCU. Hughes graduated from Lincoln University [Chester County, Pennsylvania] in 1929. Through his poetry and other writings, he provides colorful portrayals of Black life in America during the early-to-mid-20th century (Lincoln University, n.d.). Hughes is recognized as one of the leaders of the Harlem Renaissance, which was a cultural movement that focused on African American artistic expressions and the struggle for equal rights (bio, 2015).

In 1930, future U.S. Supreme Court Justice Thurgood Marshall graduated from Lincoln University. It is also important to note that Kwame Nkrumah, the Pan-Africanist and former president of Ghana, was also a student at Lincoln University, where he completed a Bachelor's degree in Sociology in 1935. In pursuit of becoming a civil rights attorney, Thurgood Marshall entered law school at Howard University and graduated magna cum laude and first in his class in 1933 (Thurgood Marshall College Fund, 2012). Marshall was greatly involved in the National Association for the Advancement of Colored People's (NAACP) initiatives aimed at challenging Jim Crow legislation and discrimination against African Americans. He is best known for his involvement in the 1954 Supreme Court case *Brown v. Board of Education*, which declared public school segregation to be unconstitutional.

Additionally, Civil Rights Leader and Nobel Peace Laureate Dr. Martin Luther King, Jr. earned a Bachelor's degree in Sociology from Morehouse College in 1948 (Morehouse College, n.d.). It is worth noting that King, who was a child prodigy, was an early-admit and only fifteen years old when he began his education at Morehouse. By graduating from Morehouse, King was also continuing a family tradition that began with his grandfather, Dr. Adam Daniel Williams, in 1898. King's own sons, Martin (III) and Dexter, are also a part of the Morehouse legacy.

Toni Morrison, the highly acclaimed novelist and educator, is also an HBCU graduate. In 1953, Morrison graduated with a Bachelor of Arts degree in English from Howard University (Washington, D.C.). Morrison has received the Pulitzer Prize, the American Book Award, and the Nobel Prize for her work *Beloved*, which is still used in many U.S. schools today. Additionally, international figure, media proprietor, talk show host, actress, producer, philanthropist, and billionaire Oprah Winfrey, received her start at Tennessee State University as a Communications major, where she completed her degree in 1973.

Other notable African Americans who have graduated from HBCUs include Herman Cain [Morehouse, 1967], Jerry Rice [Mississippi Valley State University 1984], and Shelton "Spike" Lee [Morehouse College, 1979]. And more contemporarily, several prominent African Americans completed their education at HBCUs. Tom Joyner, radio host and founder of

REACH Media, Inc., graduated from Tuskegee University with a Sociology degree in 1978. Similarly, Yolanda Adams, award-winning Gospel singer, radio show host, and actress graduated from Texas Southern University in 1983 with a degree in Radio/Television Communications. Pam Oliver, NBA and NFL sportscaster, graduated from Florida A&M University in 1983 with a Bachelor's degree in Broadcast Journalism. Jacque Reid, popular television and radio personality, earned a Bachelor's degree in Print Journalism from Clark Atlanta University in 1989. And Stephen Anthony Smith, sports journalist and ESPN personality, received a degree in Mass Communications from Winston-Salem State University in 1991 (Winston-Salem State University, n.d.).

Anika Noni Rose, Tony Award-winning singer and actress, graduated from Florida A&M University with a Bachelor's degree in Theatre in 1994 (FAMU, n.d.). Similarly, Taraji P. Henson, actress, singer, and Academy Award nominee began her college career at North Carolina A&T State University, but soon after transferred to Howard University where she completed a degree in Fine Arts in 1995. Henson has shared stories of her son being racially profiled by police at University of Southern California (McGloster, 2015). As a result, she decided to enroll him at Howard University. In addition, Keshia Knight Pulliam, a young actress most popularly known for her role as "Rudy Huxtable" on "The Cosby Show," graduated from Spelman College with a Bachelor's degree in Sociology in 2001. In 2010, Pulliam founded Kamp Kizzy, a nonprofit organization for young girls. Additionally, in 2010, child prodigy Stephen R. Stafford II joined the legacy of Dr. Martin Luther King, Jr. by enrolling at Morehouse College at the age of 13, where he is a triple major in biology, mathematics and computer science. Stafford began taking courses at Morehouse when he was 11 years old.

In spite of HBCUs' long and decorated history of educating African Americans, their future remains uncertain. More recently, schools like St. Augustine's University and South Carolina State University have been struggling to stay open amidst accreditation and financial challenges. At Elizabeth City State University in North Carolina, the enrollment has decreased by 27%. Additionally, Shaw University has more than 20 million dollars in debt (Chambers, 2015) and Barber-Scotia College lost its accreditation in 2004. Over the last 80 years, several HBCUs have closed, these closings include: Daniel Payne College [1889–1977], Friendship College [1891–1981], Guadalupe College [1884-1936], Kittrell College [1886–1975], Leland College [1870–1960], Mississippi Industrial College [1905–1982)], Western University (Kansas) [1865–1943], Prentiss Institute

[1907–1989], Bishop College [1881–1988], Natchez Junior College [1884–1989], Mary Holmes College [1892–2004], and South Carolina State University [on probationary status and proposed to temporarily close until 2017]. Schools like Morris Brown College, Howard, Clarke Atlanta, Fisk, Cheyney, Tennessee State, and Wilberforce Universities, among others, continue to face accreditation and or financial struggles.

These institutions are faced with contemporary challenges that include: declining Black student enrollment, financial instability, accreditation sanctions, and increasing speculations concerning the value of an HBCU degree in the 21st century. Additionally, in consideration of the fact that the mission of HBCUs are changing in order to accommodate greater racial diversity, the need to sustain federal and state funding has had an impact on the enrollment of these institutions. Enrollment trends over the 20th—and now 21st century, are indicative of how integration has both positively and negatively impacted HBCUs. Notwithstanding the social, political and economic changes in the American landscape, HBCUs continue to play an important role in African American higher education attainment (NCES, 2012), and they are some of the leading producers of Black science, technology, engineering and mathematics graduates (Upton & Tanenbaum, 2014). In this sense, these institutions are *the titans* or *giants of Black higher education*. However, because of the gradual decline in Black enrollment at these institutions, there is a need to more deeply examine the relevance of these schools in the 21st century.

It is in this light that this book explores the historical and contemporary role of HBCUs in the education of African Americans. While this is not intended to be an exhaustive treatment on the topic, the book examines how HBCUs have served—and continue to serve as a force in Black higher education. The book presents a case study of African American high school students' perceptions about attending an HBCU. Since these are the prospective students who are most likely to attend a Black institution of higher education, we explore the following research question: *What are the perceptions of African American college-bound students on attending a Historically Black College or University*?

In the context of this book, the following terms are operationalized.

HISTORICALLY BLACK COLLEGE OR UNIVERSITY (HBCU)

HBCUs are degree-granting institutions that were established in the 1800s and prior to 1964, with the principal mission of providing educational access and opportunities for African Americans. While HBCUs have traditionally and contemporarily served mainly African Americans, enrollment is open to all students regardless of their race or ethnicity. These schools are categorized as: public 2- and 4-year colleges/universities, private 4-year colleges/universities, and land-grant institutions. There are approximately 100 HBCUs [public and private] across the nation that confer associates, bachelors, and advanced-level degrees.

PREDOMINATELY WHITE INSTITUTION (PWI)

A predominantly White institution (PWI) is a postsecondary college or university with White students accounting for 50% or more of the student body. These institutions are considered historically White and are most commonly rooted with patterns and traditions of Western Europe.

AFRICAN AMERICANS/BLACKS

An African American is someone who is of African descent which can include being born in the U.S., but having African ancestral lineage. Additionally, this term is also inclusive of immigrant born Blacks, that is, people who are of African descent and now reside in – or outside of continental Africa. In this book, the term *African Americans* is used interchangeably with *Blacks*. Due to the historical and contemporary nature of the book's topic, we do not differentiate between the two terms.

In chapter 1, we provide a background on the pre-colonial entry of Africans into the Americas, as well as African educational traditions, and the struggles for education during the period of enslavement in North America. In the second chapter, we discuss the social, historical and contemporary context that pertains to the development of Black education and the formation of HBCUs as a framework for our study. In the third chapter, we introduce our study on African American college-bound students' perceptions about attending an HBCU. And in the final chapter, we discuss our findings and provide recommendations regarding the future of HBCUs.

CHAPTER 1

LAST OF THE BLACK TITANS

Background on the entry of Africans in the Americas

The entry of Africans into the Americas dates back to 800 B.C.E., before the arrival of Europeans. During this time, Africans who were later called Olmecs sailed to the Americas. Artifacts from their civilization have been discovered by modern researchers. The Olmecs had a presence throughout the Americas and particularly in Mexico (See Ivan Van Sertima's *They Came Before Columbus* and Robin Walker's *When We Ruled; The Ancient and Medieval History of Black Civilizations*). While in the Americas, they developed a relationship with other native groups such as the Aztecs, Mayans, Caribs, Tainos, Chibchas, Tupis, Guaranis, Incas, Araucanians, and the Arawaks, among others. Back in Africa, African societies varied from communal hunter-gather societies to advanced civilizations (Diop, 1974). Africans also had educational traditions on the continent of Africa. In fact, the early development of institutions of higher education is attributed to—and directly linked to continental Africa and historical Egypt (also known as Kemet, meaning the land of the Blacks). Obenga (1992) asserts that, "a crucial understanding of the transmission of knowledge can be understood by the direct line that the Greek educational lineage inherited from Kemet" (p. 21). He further postulates that, "this is why we are interested in African philosophy of the Pharaonic period: to connect the contemporary with that of the ancient and to demonstrate the pre-existence of African philosophy before its appearance anywhere else on this earth" (p. 28). On this issue the ancient Greek Plutarch, in his book *Parallel Lives*, notes: "The 'wisdom of the Egyptians' always seems to have a fascination for the Greeks, and at this period Alexandria, with its famous library and its memories of the Ptolemies, of Kallimachus and of Theokritus, was an important [center] of Greek intellectual activity" (Plutarch, 75 C.E./2012, p. 17). Similarly, Greek Historian Herodotus in his *Histories* explain:

> For the people of Colchis are evidently Egyptian, and this I perceived for myself before I heard it from others. So when I had come to consider the matter I asked them both; and the Colchians had remembrance of the

> Egyptians more than the Egyptians of the Colchians; but the Egyptians said they believed that the Colchians were a portion of the army of Sesostris. That this was so I conjectured myself not only because they are dark-skinned and have curly hair, but also still more because the Colchians, Egyptians, and Ethiopians alone of all the races of men have [practiced] circumcision from the first. (Herodotus, 440 B.C.E./2014, *Second book of the histories,* section 104)

Herodotus continues:

> But as to those matters which concern men, the priests agreed with one another in saying that the Egyptians were the first of all men on earth to find out the course of the year, having divided the seasons into twelve parts to make up the hole; and this they said they found out from the stars: and they reckon to this extent more wisely than the Hellenes… (Herodotus, 440 B.C.E./2014, *Second book of the histories*, section 4)

To the extent and acknowledgment of Plutarch, Herodotus and others regarding the intellectual tradition and contributions of Black Africans, it should be recognized that access to—and further development of knowledge for African Americans in a contemporary sense is rather an inherited right from their ancestral beginnings, because people of African descent have been creators and transmitters of knowledge since its inception. In fact, two of the oldest universities in the world, the University of Waset and the University of Sankore were located in continental Africa (African Kingdoms, n.d.). In 1280, the University at Timbuktu in West Africa (also called University of Sankore) was created under Mansa Musa's reign, who was the King of Mali (Davidson, 1964). Mansa Musa was one of the wealthiest kings of the Medieval World. Saad (1983) explains that the ancient city of Timbuktu and its institutions of higher learning were created by Africans who converted to Islam. These Africans maintained a tradition of scholarly excellence. Saad (1983) notes:

> Although it was not uncommon to engage in several fields of study at the same time, candidates to scholarship usually began their higher education in grammar, then in *tafsir*. In Qur'anic literacy school (*mak-tabs*), these two fields at an elementary level were treated as one and the same; the instructor (*mu'allim*) introduced his students to Arabic grammar while teaching and dictating the text of the Qur'an itself. At more advanced levels, the two fields were likewise studied simultaneously, though sometimes under different masters. The

> main distinction lay in the fact that the students were introduced to grammatical commentaries as such, while in *tafsir*, works of a wide range of authorities were used as textbooks. (p. 74)

Saad's (1983) findings are also supported by the narrative of al-Hasan ibn Muhammad al-Wazzan al-Fasi (also known as Leo Africanus). In 1518, Spanish soldiers captured al-Hasan ibn Muhammad al-Wazzan al-Fasi, a Muslim scholar of Moorish descent (an African descendent living in Granada, Spain). Once the Spanish learned of al-Wassan al Fasi's brilliance as a scholar, they presented him to Pope Leo X as a gift. Pope Leo X had al-Wassan al-Fasi baptized into Roman Catholicism and changed his name to Leo Africanus. This was perhaps a strategic move by Africanus to save his own life. Pope Leo commissioned Africanus to write a book that described and explained the contours of North Africa. Africanus' book was entitled, *Description of Africa,* or also called, *The History and Description of Africa: And of the Notable Things Therein Contained* (BBC: Leo Africanus, 2011). In the *Description of Africa,* Africanus makes the following observation:

> Passing therefore westward from the Island of Siene, you enter into the prouince of Nubia, bordering on the west upon Gaoga, eastward upon the riuer Nilus, towards the North, upon Egypt, and southward upon the desert of Goran. The inhabitants thereof called by *Strabo* liue at this present (as Francisco Aluarez reporteth) a most miserable and wretched kinde of life; for hauing lost the sincerities and light of the gospel, they do embrace infinite corruption of the Iewish and Mahumetan religions[1]...
>
> Meroe called at this time by the names of Guengare, Amara, and Nobe, being the greatest and fairest isle which Nilus maketh, and resembled by Herodotus to the shape of a target, containeth in bredth a thousand, and in length three thousand stadios or furlongs. (Africanus, Pory, & Brown, 1600, pp. 28–29)

Africanus' knowledge would prove to be most valuable to European nations and explorers who were interested in carving up and colonizing the continent of Africa (Wiggan, 2015). The narrative of Leo Africanus points to the fact that Africans were literate before the arrival of Europeans. However, they had literacy in their own social and cultural context, which was not always valued in the Eurocentric western world, particularly on the plantations of the Americas.

Clarke (1977) provides insight on the intentional and neglected intellectual history of African scholarship. When elaborating on the University of Sankore, Clarke (1977) explains:

> Before the destruction of the Empire of Songhay by the Moroccans and European mercenary soldiers at the end of the sixteenth century, the Africans in the Western Sudan (inner East Africa) had been bringing into being great empires and cultures for over a thousand years, the most notable empires being Ghana and Mali. The Songhay Empire and the University of Sankore, at Timbuctoo, was in existence over a hundred years after the slave trade had already been started along the west coast of Africa. During this period in West African history–from the early part of the fourteenth century to the time of the Moorish invasion in 1591–the city of Timbuctoo and the University of Sankore in the Songhay Empire were the intellectual centers of Africa. Black scholars were enjoying a renaissance that was known and respected throughout most of Africa and in parts of Europe. (Clarke, 1977, p. 142)

To this extent, the notion of Greeks being the creators of philosophy and intellectual thought as postulated in Western academies, should be dispelled. Clarke (1977) and many others [i.e., Asa Hilliard, John G. Jackson, Molefi Asante, Marimba Ani, etc.] have attempted to correct these forms of miseducation through their scholarship in fields such as Africana Studies, Anthropology, History, Kemetology (Egyptology) and Sociology in order to realign philosophical, methodological, historical, and intellectual thought towards continental Africa–where education and civilization began. In fact, a 2013 study conducted at the University of Illinois at Urbana Champaign sought to determine what percent of U.S. colleges and universities offer African American studies programs. The findings revealed that currently 76% of U.S. colleges and universities provide some form of Black Studies (Alkalimat et al., 2013). However, only 20% of these institutions had formal units or programs, while 56% reported that they offered Black Studies through a course or a series of courses (Alkalimat et al., 2013). While many schools did not have official Black Studies Departments, they reported that they offered this curriculum through departmental units or elective courses (Alkalimat et al., 2013). This is a tribute to the legacy of William Leo Hansberry, who established the first Black Studies/Africana Studies program in the U.S. at Howard University in 1922. However, the struggle to correct the curriculum and to infuse multicultural and diversity perspectives in public K-12 education and PWIs is ongoing, as education is one of the last great battlefields for freedom and democracy.

Notwithstanding these educational developments in continental Africa and Black education in the U.S., as noted, the historical period of Africans' involuntary entry and enslavement in North America began in 1619 with the arrival of African slaves (also called indentured servants) taken from the island of Barbados to James Town, Virginia. This marked the beginning of one of the greatest atrocities in human history, and whose impact, consequences and outcomes are still lingering in the 21st century (See John Henrik Clarke's *Christopher Columbus and the Afrikan Holocaust*). After the events of 1619, Africans would later be taken directly from the continent of Africa to North America in chattel slavery, where they were bought, sold, traded, and bred like cattle for profits. As early as 1644, a group of Boston businessmen financed three slave ships to sail directly to Africa. As the profits and competition for slaves increased, conflicts between Protestant and Catholic countries became intense. Since North America was established as a Protestant country under British colonialism, it developed its own local and global economy based principally on slavery, sharecropping, and trading spices. Internationally, the enslavement of Africans played a crucial role in the development of global capitalism (see Eric Williams' *Capitalism and Slavery*). The struggle for freedom would continue throughout the Civil War [1861–1865] and into the Reconstruction period [1865–1877].

Prior to the Reconstruction period, the time that followed the American Civil War, most African Americans (termed as "Negroes") were in positions of servitude and they were not permitted to receive a formal education. It was illegal for a slave to learn how to read and write for this would threaten the White establishment and the institution of slavery (Woodson, 1915). For example, in 1740, South Carolina officially passed the Negro Act, which was formal legislation that made it illegal to teach African Americans to read English. As noted above, the Africans were literate in their native languages, practices, and culture. However, by 1835, most southern and many northern states had officially passed anti-literacy laws. For example, as early as 1641, Massachusetts was among the first colonies to legalize slavery, and as a rule, slaves were not permitted to learn to read.

Similarly, in 1667 in the state of Virginia, a law was passed that indicated that Christian baptism did not change a Black person's status as a slave. In other words, even if the enslaved Africans converted to Christianity, they were to remain as slaves (PBS, 2004). Slaveholders were interested in

Christianizing slaves and keeping them illiterate; this included giving them Protestant names, changing their cultural ethos to Europeanize them, and teaching them to be obedient and to wait until the 'afterlife' to receive their reward for being good servants.

Thus, the pursuit of education became evermore important for African Americans after slavery because it served as a promise for freedom and racial uplift (Wiggan, Scott, Watson, & Reynolds, 2014). With the help of empathetic northern Whites and through the work of the American Colonization Society, a controversial White organization that sought to train and relocate *free* Blacks to Liberia to help run an American colony in Africa, a small, but select group of African Americans received a college degree before the Civil War (see Carter G. Woodson's *The Education of the Negro prior to 1861*). Through these and other deliberate, but dangerous attempts at providing an education to African Americans, there was a small group of educated Blacks before the Civil War. For example, in 1849 Charles Lewis Reason became the first Black faculty member on a White college campus in America. He was a professor of mathematics at New York Central College in McGrawville, New York (Wiggan, 2011). Additionally, the distinguished scholar Martin Henry Freeman graduated from Middlebury College in 1849 and he remained in Vermont and later became a professor at Avery College (formerly Allegheny Institute). Among other Black professors were William G. Allen and George B. Vashon who both served at Avery College in the 1860s. And later, in 1876, Edward Alexander Bouchet graduated from Yale University with a Ph.D. in physics, making him the first African American to receive a doctorate from an American university (Wiggan, 2010).

After the Reconstruction period [1865–1877] and landmark legislation (such as *Brown v. Board of Education* in 1954) pushing for the development of education for all Americans, the introduction of new educational opportunities greatly influenced Black students' decision to attend HBCUs. With the aftermath of the Civil War, HBCUs represented one of the few opportunities for African Americans to receive access to higher education (Jackson, 2001; Lovett, 2011). In the *College Bred Negro American*, W. E. B. Du Bois explained the impact of Black college graduates at the turn of the 20th century. Du Bois argued that HBCUs played a vital role in the production of Black college graduates and Black leaders. For Du Bois' monumental intellectual contributions to Black social progress, Historian John Henrik Clarke has rightly referred to him as a Black titan (see John Henrik Clarke et al.'s *Black titan: W.E.B. Du Bois*). Similarly, with respect to the impact of historically black colleges and universities, at the institutional level one might argue that HBCUs were *titans* or *giants of Black education* and Black social progress. In this book, *Black titans* is used to underscore the significant role that HBCUs have—and continue to play in the education of African Americans.

While having rich institutional legacies, during the early-to-mid 20th century, with increased resistance against segregation and gradual advances in the integration of PWIs, African Americans' enrollment at HBCUs began to decline. According to data from the National Center for Education Statistics (NCES), there was a continual decline in African American student enrollment in HBCUs that started in the early part of the 20th century (NCES, 1995, 2004). From the second-half of the 20th century to 2015, there have been several prevailing factors that have threatened the future of HBCUs: (a) looming financial issues (Cantey, Bland, Mack, & Joy-Davis, 2012; Minor, 2008; Stuart, 2012), (b) accreditation concerns (Fester, Gasman, & Nguyen, 2012), and (c) negative media attention (Gasman, 2006, 2007; Gasman & Bowman, 2011; Jencks & Riesman, 1967). Although HBCUs have played a major role (both historically and contemporarily) in the education of African Americans (Albritton, 2012; Anderson, 1988; Cantey et al., 2012; Franklin & Savage, 2004; Freeman, 1999; Kim & Conrad, 2006; Perna, 2001; Thompson, 2008; Wiggan, 2011; Woodson, 1915), one is left to wonder about the continuing significance of these *Black titans* in the 21st century. If HBCUs are looking to African Americans as their primary constituency for their enrollment, then it should be imperative that these institutions obtain feedback on how this demographic views these schools when considering which college or university to attend. Today, HBCUs enroll between 9% and 10% of all African Americans attending a college or university, and they award approximately 20% of all Black students' undergraduate degrees (Thurgood Marshall Fund, 2015; UNCF, 2014).

A growing body of literature explains HBCUs' historical and continuing contributions to the African American community (Anderson, 1988; Davis, 1998; Franklin & Savage, 2004; Jackson, 2001; Wiggan, 2011). Many researchers attribute HBCUs with providing students with cultural value, social empowerment, and the development of racial and cultural identities (Brown, Ricard, & Donahoo, 2004; Franklin & Savage, 2004; Lovett, 2011). These institutional characteristics are consistently identified as being part of an HBCU experience. It should then be recognized that Black students who attend HBCUs participate in what shall be termed as a *Black college experience*, an issue that is addressed later in this book [Chapter 3]. Davis

(2006) discusses the Black college experience as one that is characteristic of institutional family, cultural immersion, and universal inclusion. That is, in the Black college setting, students feel more connected to the faculty, staff, and their peers through social activities and organizations, all of which help to solidify common cultural values and social bonds. This book seeks to explore African American college-bound teens' perceptions about selecting and attending an HBCU. It addresses the need to investigate how student perceptions are related to HBCU enrollment in the 21st century.

CONTEMPORARY ISSUES FACING HBCUS

HBCUs are credited with producing 50% of the Black school teachers and administrators (Thurgood Marshall College Fund, 2015). These success rates can be attributed to the nurturing and supporting environment at these institutions. However, perceptions surrounding the contemporary role of these institutions continue to challenge their stability. In this sense, HBCUs were perceived as important when African Americans were unable to gain access to higher education at other institutions. However, more recently, many question if HBCUs are still relevant since African American students generally have options as it relates to accessing higher education. In addition to decreased enrollment, school finances (Cantey et al., 2012; Minor, 2008; Stuart, 2012), negative media attention (Gasman & Bowman, 2011), and accreditation concerns (Fester et al., 2012) are some of the issues that HBCUs must mediate.

Minor (2008) discusses the issues related to HBCUs in regards to financial challenges, anti-affirmative action policies, and competition from PWIs and community colleges. Minor (2008) explains that much of the confusion about the role of HBCUs rested on where they were historically and what they are becoming in the contemporary era. Historically, HBCUs principally served African Americans. However, today, with pressure from governors and state legislatures to close or diversify these schools, affirmative action is now used at public HBCUs for White students, to help bring diversity to these institutions (meaning more non-Black students) (Paddock, 2013). This is affirmative action for White students. HBCUs like Delaware State University and Winston-Salem State University have increased their enrollment of White students, many of whom are attending on scholarships and or affirmative action related tuition waivers. While the historical use of affirmative action is shifting to encourage White students to attend HBCUs, some opponents of these initiatives see HBCUs—or any institution that is premised and operated to serve a racial minority student population, as unnecessary and unjustifiable in the 21st century. Still, HBCUs represent an important pathway that helps provide African Americans with access to postsecondary education. Minor (2008) argues that three elements are needed to understand the contemporary role of HBCUs: (a) assessment of enrollment trends over the last few decades; (b) legal sanctions that have impacted HBCU infrastructures; and (c) the relationship that racial context has as a variable in education attainment. He asserts that despite Civil Rights triumphs, many states have still found ways to segregate higher education opportunities.

For example, Mississippi has restricted access by race to state colleges by promoting disparities in admission policies, academic programs, and funding (Minor, 2008). Specifically, "other race" degree policies, or funding tied to increasing non-Black student enrollment at HBCUs, have negatively impacted student enrollment (Minor, 2008). Given such racially restrictive school funding measures, Minor (2008) contends that the survival of HBCUs will depend on how successful these institutions are in convincing the public that their mission is still important.

National Center for Education Statistics data from 2004 and 2012 (NCES, 2013) indicate that nationally, college enrollment for African Americans has increased, specifically at PWIs. Among public HBCUs, African Americans are still the largest student population. However, as NCES (2013) data reveals, the number of African American students entering and attending HBCUs is gradually declining (see Table 1). Cantey, Bland, Mack, and Joy-Davis (2012) concur and acknowledge that decreasing enrollment must be countered with new initiatives in technology, the recruitment and retention of high quality faculty, and by modeling Black success through increasing the presence of African American faculty who hold PhDs. Matthews and Hawkins (2006) note that HBCU administrators and leaders should showcase how these institutions are adjusting and thriving, in spite of their challenges. They note:

> Despite their problems—fractured budgets, ailing and aging infrastructures, and revolving door leadership—they continue to do more with less while managing to outpace majority institutions in training and producing the majority of the nation's Black teachers, preachers, social workers, lawyers, doctors, journalists, engineers, and scholars. (Matthews & Hawkins, 2006, p. 37)

Although HBCUs have a legacy of nurturing Black student success, the future of these institutions is at risk. In the next chapter, we discuss the social context that pertains to the development of Black education and the formation of Black institutions of higher learning as a framework for our investigation on 21st century high school students' perceptions about attending an HBCU.

NOTE

1 It is important to note that at the time of Africanus' writing, the letter "J" was not created as yet.

CHAPTER 2

HISTORICAL AND SOCIAL CONTEXT OF EDUCATION FOR AFRICAN AMERICANS

To understand how HBCUs contribute to African American education, the historical and social context of Black education must be explored. As noted in the previous chapter, the involuntary entry of African Americans into North America dates back to 1619, the year that slaves (indentured servants) from Barbados were transported to Jamestown, Virginia. Since Barbados was also a British colony, these Africans were bought, sold and transplanted by the Dutch West India Company from one slave colony into another. As profits from slavery increased, dehumanization created racial stratification and the ongoing linkage of Black skin to enslavement (Anderson, 1988; Woodson, 1915).

In this context of evolving racism, Historian and Educator Carter G. Woodson (1915) discussed Black education. Woodson divided pre-emancipation or the pre-1861 era into two periods: (a) the introduction of slavery when debates ensued regarding whether slaves should be educated, and (b), the Industrial Revolution where slavery transitioned into an economic institution where African Americans organized attempts, in spite of servitude, to be educated and freed. During what Woodson called the Industrial Revolution era, White advocates of education for African Americans belonged to one of the following groups: (a) businessmen who stood to economically benefit from a vocationally trained labor force, (b) reformers/abolitionists who wanted to help enslaved and free born African descendant people, or (c) those looking to proselytize slaves into Christianity (Anderson, 1988; Woodson, 1915). Woodson (1915) recalled:

> With all of these new opportunities Negroes exhibited a rapid mental development. Intelligent colored men proved to be useful and trustworthy servants; they became much better laborers and artisans, and many of them showed administrative ability adequate to the management of business establishments and large plantations. Moreover, better rudimentary education served many ambitious persons of color as a stepping stone–to higher attainments. Negroes learned to appreciate and write poetry and contributed something to mathematics, science,

> and philosophy. Furthermore, having disproved the theories of their mental inferiority, some of the race, in conformity with the suggestion of Cotton Mather, were employed to teach white children. (p. 5)

As the number of educated African Americans increased, the effort to establish schools specifically for Black children grew. These schools provided courses relevant to the employment needs of Whites, which were premised on manual labor. Between 1619 and 1865, there were empathetic Whites who taught some slaves how to read and write the English language. African American slaves who could read and write could also teach other slaves to read. However, White settlers who stood in opposition to Black education argued that if slavery was to continue, slaves would have to remain in the lowest state of ignorance (Anderson, 1988). The rise of production and plantation crops in the South called for more slaves, and many Southerners decided that it would be more profitable to work slaves until their death, rather than teaching them how to read and write (Woodson, 1915).

Fugitive slaves and freed Blacks who lived in the northern states organized themselves to gain access to schools. Their efforts yielded considerable challenges to their presumed status as citizens with the right to public education. At the same time, White Christian ministers provided learning opportunities in the form of rote memorization of Bible verses and religious instruction (Anderson, 1988; Morgan, 1995; Woodson, 1915). These learning techniques quickly spread and those who opposed the education of Blacks became even more aggressive with passing legislation prohibiting any form of instruction for "Negroes." It is fitting to mention here that as early as 1740, North Carolina passed legislation that prohibited slaves from learning to read the English language. In spite of these attempts to prevent African Americans from being literate and obtaining an education, abolitionists continued to defy these laws because adhering to them would only obstruct their own efforts to either have an efficient labor force or disseminate teachings of Christianity (Anderson, 1988).

With the spread of Christianity, less concerted efforts were made to breakup secret schools (See Thomas Webber's *Deep like the rivers: Education in the slave quarter communities*). These were schools that were created by African Americans and were hidden from plantation owners, where they taught each other how to read and write (Woodson, 1915). Some plantation owners and White settlers observed that those who could read the Bible and learn the scriptures remained loyal and subordinate to their slaveholders because they were generally taught to be submissive (Woodson, 1915). In this sense,

White missionaries played a key part in teaching African Americans to read so that they could learn from the Bible (Anderson, 1988; Jackson, 2001; Watkins, 2001).

The physical and mental bonds of slavery posed limitations on African Americans' access to formal education. However, Anderson (1988) explains that slaves remained persistent by teaching each other in secret and creating their own schools. Additionally, some liberal White colleges in the northern states provided educational opportunities for Blacks prior to the Reconstruction period. Most notably, Alexander Lucius Twilight was the first African American to receive a college degree in North America. He graduated from Middlebury College in Vermont in 1823 (Journal of Blacks in Higher Education [JBHE], 2013). Additionally, in 1826, Edward Jones was the first African American graduate of Amherst College in Massachusetts (Amherst College, n.d.), and in that same year, John Brown Russwurm became the first Black graduate of Bowdoin College in Maine (Bowdoin College Library, n.d.). These were the first three African descent people to receive a college degree in North America. After the Civil War, several African Americans received advanced degrees. For example, Edward Bouchet [Yale University, 1876], Eva B. Dykes [Radcliffe College, 1921 (Radcliffe later merged with Harvard University)], Sadie Tanner Mossell Alexander [University of Pennsylvania, 1921], and Georgiana R. Simpson [University of Chicago, 1921] all serve as exemplars for being the first African Americans to earn doctorate degrees (JBHE, n.d.). It is important to mention that Eva B. Dykes, Sadie Tanner Mossell Alexander and Georgiana R. Simpson were the first African American women to earn PhDs in the U.S., which is a part of the decorated history of Blacks in higher education.

FORMATION OF SCHOOLS FOR AFRICAN AMERICANS

During the period of the Civil War [1861 to1865], African Americans were recruited as soldiers by promising them freedom in exchange for their service. However, those freedoms were deferred. Therefore, the 13th Amendment was important in ending slavery, the 14th Amendment provided greater legal rights for African Americans, and the 15th Amendment of the U.S. Constitution granted African Americans the right to vote. The Emancipation Proclamation [1863] itself—had given African Americans in the South opportunities to begin establishing themselves as free citizens. However, there was still great discontent in the southern states. In fact, many Blacks in the South did not find out that they were free until two-and-a-half-years after the Emancipation Proclamation was signed (History of Juneteenth, n.d.). For example, in Texas, slavery continued to thrive because slaves had no knowledge of their freedom because it took longer for the Union soldiers to enter the state, which was a slavery stronghold. Slave owners were deliberate about keeping their slaves illiterate and denying them an education. Thus, Anderson (1988) explains that ex-slaves coming out of the Civil War were the first to "crusade for the state systems of common schools" (p. 148) for Black children. This was more common in the northern and New England states, because in the South, African Americans were met with the greatest forms of opposition from Whites, which included even paying the highest price of facing death. While even risking their lives, African Americans continued their pursuit for education.

Around 1865 in Atlanta, Georgia two former slaves, James Tate and Grandison B. Daniels, founded a small private school for African Americans in an African Methodist Episcopal church building on the corner of Courtland and Jenkins streets in Atlanta (AU Collection, 1800s). This was a one-room school where students ranged from ages 5–16. The belief in education and the ideas of education for freedom and self-help were firmly established by Tate and Daniels. The duo founded the first Black school in Atlanta, Georgia, which subsequently led to the founding of Atlanta University once northern missionaries moved to the South (Wiggan, 2011). It was not until the end of the 19th century that Black children were given access to public elementary school education in the South. Anderson (1988) argues that resources for Black education were limited because public school funds (money collected through taxation) were being allocated primarily to White schools for White children.

The Freedmen's Bureau in particular, along with northern philanthropists, helped to establish formal schooling and education for Black children in the South (Anderson, 1988; Morgan, 1995; Watkins, 2001). Originally known as the U.S. Bureau of Refugees, Freedmen, and Abandoned Lands, the Freedmen's Bureau helped to establish more than 4,000 schools for African Americans (Holmes, 1934; Jackson, 2001). White religious organizations were also instrumental in creating education of African Americans. Watkins (2001) elaborates:

> They were a part of the cultural and religious evolution of the South, they accepted an evolutionary view of societal change, they espoused the paternal social and racial relations of the South, they accepted the emergent corporate-industrial economic arrangements as modernization, and they were willing and eager participants in educating minorities. Although accepting of America's economic order,

> the missionary leaders were fervent believers in education as a tool for racial advancement. (p. 15)

In addition to the work of White missionary societies, northern philanthropists also played a key role in Black education. However, they had a clear motive in doing so. Anderson (1988) argues that northern philanthropists were purposeful in providing training only for industrial labor, which would provide skilled workers for the new economy without challenging the White establishment (Wiggan, 2011). Additionally, Watkins (2001) argues that philanthropic efforts were really intended to exercise political and social ideology related to social servitude (and dominance) over African Americans.

Anderson and Moss (1999) note:

> Philanthropists created and supported schools, argue some scholars, as a means to achieve larger goals, particularly the maintenance of social peace after the Civil War and the creation of a class of submissive workers. (p. 1)

Still, with the combined efforts of the independent Black church, Freedmen's Bureau, White missionary organizations, and northern philanthropists, HBCUs began to emerge to help educate African Americans. Most notably, in 1867, Howard University was established as a Black institution of higher learning through a charter by the U.S. Congress. In 1868, the Hampton Normal and Agricultural Institute (currently known as Hampton University) was founded by Samuel Chapman Armstrong and the American Missionary Association (AMA) (Anderson & Moss, 1999; Fields & Murty, 2012; Jackson, 2001). Other schools formed by the AMA included: Atlanta University [1865], Fisk University [1866], Talladega College [1867], and Tugaloo Institute [1869], among others (Anderson, 1988; Fields & Murty, 2012; Wiggan, 2011).

The American Baptist Home Mission Society, which was established in 1824, was also instrumental in starting schools. The organization's main mission was to "preach the gospel, establish churches and support ministry among the unchurched and destitute" (American Baptist Home Mission Society, 2007, para. 2). In 1867, this organization founded the Augusta Theological Institute in Augusta (currently known as Morehouse College). The American Baptist Home Mission Society also founded: Virginia Union University [1865], Shaw University [1865], and Benedict College [1870], among others (Fields & Murty, 2012). Additionally, the Methodist Episcopal (ME) Church helped to establish Rust College in 1866 and Morgan State College in 1867 (currently Morgan State University) (Anderson, 1988; Fields & Murty, 2012). During the Reconstruction period, northern ME churches supported school initiatives for African Americans. Prior to the Reconstruction period, disputes between northern and southern ME Church leaders over slavery created conflicts and tensions (Carwardine, 2000). Despite the American Baptist Home Mission Society and the ME churches' contributions in promoting postsecondary education for African Americans, it is important to note that most Black schools relied on the Freedmen's Bureau, AMA, northern philanthropists, and the independent Black church for financial support.

With regards to Black church groups and the formation of HBCUs, the African Methodist Episcopal Church (AME) and specifically, Bishop Richard Allen, have been recognized for providing higher educational opportunities for African Americans across the nation (Wiggan, 2011). In this sense, HBCUs were *titans* in Black education. In addition to Allen serving as a chief leader of the AME Church, he also developed the African Society for the Education of Youth (African American Registry, 2000). Some of the institutions established by the AME Church included Wilberforce University [1856], Edward Waters College [1866], Allen University [1870], Paul Quinn College [1872], Morris Brown College [1881], and Xavier University [1915], among others (Fields & Murty, 2012; Jackson, 2001). The African Methodist Episcopal Zion Church (AMEZ) also established Livingstone College, Clinton Junior College, and Lomax-Hannon College, among other schools (Fields & Murty, 2012; Watkins, 2001). Finally, institutions such as Lane College, Paine College, Texas College, and Miles Memorial College (Miles College) were founded by the Colored Methodist Episcopal (CME) Church (Anderson, 1988). The aims of these institutions were to produce Black leaders and educators, as well as to promote religious and spiritual education, and to help students develop a sense of social responsibility.

Much like the missionary groups, philanthropy was also important for HBCUs. Watkins (2001) notes:

> Race philanthropy was ideally suited to educating Blacks as well as other minorities. The building and support of schools, the training of teachers, and, very important, the construction of curriculum could be accomplished handily by corporate philanthropies. (p. 19)

The Slater Fund, Rosenwald Fund, Peabody Education Fund, Rockefeller Fund, Carnegie Fund, and many others, provided financial support to HBCUs as a means of creating a new skilled workforce. As a result, the donors' political and ideological perspectives on Black education were transmitted through White supported HBCUs, which privileged vocational training. In fact, there was a division between northern philanthropists and missionary organizations. Most philanthropists supported industrial education, while most missionary societies favored both industrial and classical liberal arts education, which would provide African Americans with greater opportunities in the broader society (Anderson, 1988).

Following the Reconstruction period, public HBCUs (schools funded by state and federal monies) were formed primarily to provide industrial, agricultural, and mechanical training for African Americans. Yet, these schools did not initially confer liberal arts degrees. Public HBCUs were also created to prevent African Americans from attending White land-grant colleges and universities which had received federal funding through the First Morrill Act in 1862 (Fields & Murty, 2012; Library of Congress, n.d.). However, the Second Morrill Act of 1890 required states with segregated higher education systems to provide land-grant institutions for African Americans. Additionally, the U.S. Supreme Court case *Plessy v. Ferguson* in 1896, mandated that states provide separate but equal education for African Americans. This, however, never was the case. Thomas (1997) elaborates:

> Legally, the case created precedent for a comprehensive set of laws that regulated the lives of "whites" and "coloreds" in the South until 1954. Its symbolic importance is harder to determine, but clearly when the highest court in the land ruled that states could claim that legislation separating the races promoted the public good, it sent a message that African Americans would find little support from the federal judiciary. (p. 170)

In understanding the historical and racial context of this case, *Plessy v. Ferguson* justified the need for—and established formation of the NAACP (n.d.), an organization dedicated to overturning segregation and racially-biased laws and social practices in the U.S. Additionally, this case was particularly important in the fight to provide access and opportunity through public HBCUs, since African Americans were generally being denied admission to PWIs. Throughout the 19th and early-to-mid 20th century, African Americans viewed HBCUs as a social force in Black education (Anderson, 1988; Morgan, 1995; Wiggan, 2011).

Jackson (2001) notes that by 1880, nationally, only 30% of the Black population was literate. Thus, HBCUs played a key role in the production of school teachers and administrators. In 1880, there were more than 40 higher education institutions for African Americans (both private and public) spread out across the nation. HBCUs were categorized as: public 2- and 4-year colleges/universities, private 4-year colleges/universities, and land-grant institutions. The ways in which these institutions were categorized were directly related to their funding sources. That is, many private institutions began—and continue to operate with the support of philanthropic efforts and or religious institutions, whereas others are funded by the state through land-grants or other public funds.

As noted, by 1900, approximately 2,600 African Americans had postsecondary credentials, largely due to the efforts of public and private HBCUs. However, only 55% of African Americans were considered literate (Jackson, 2001). And in 1909, W. E. B. Du Bois reported that there were a total of 3,856 African American college graduates in the U.S. (Du Bois & Dill, 1910). Thus, there was a movement among Black intellectuals advocating to increase the number of Black college graduates, and they viewed HBCUs as playing a key role in this endeavor. Notable scholars such as W. E. B. Du Bois, Alain Locke, and Carter G. Woodson emerged to form a new group of Black intellectuals and leaders. Additionally, organizations such as the NAACP in 1909 and the National Urban League in 1910, were founded in order to advocate for African American education and civil rights. In 1915, Carter G. Woodson initiated the Association for the Study of Negro Life and History (currently in operation today as the Association for the Study of African American Life and History). Shortly thereafter, in 1916, began the publication of *The Journal of Negro History,* which is now the *Journal of African American History* (Jackson, 2001). By 1927, there were 77 Black colleges and universities and over 14,000 students enrolled (Jackson, 2001). In 1944, the United Negro College Fund (UNCF), a consortium of 39 private HBCUs, was incorporated with the main purpose of providing scholarships to students, raising funds for member institutions, and enhancing the overall quality of education for Black college attendees (United Negro College Fund, n.d.).

NATIONAL INITIATIVES AND HBCU ENROLLMENT

Although there were initiatives for HBCUs and recruitment aimed at increasing student enrollment, challenges pertaining to educational access and opportunities were still pervasive. As early as 1787, a group of Black Bostonians petitioned to the Massachusetts legislature to rally for common school education for their children (Martin, 1998). Within the northern region, this act and many others during this era, helped to position the *Roberts v. City of Boston* case of 1849, which sought to help African Americans gain access to Boston common schools (Martin, 1998). Following *Plessy v. Ferguson* of 1896 (as discussed earlier), in the 1950 *Sweatt v. Painter* case, Heman Marion Sweatt, a Black student who was denied access to enroll in a Texas law school, challenged the separate but equal doctrine. In the same year, the court case *McLaurin v. Oklahoma State Regents* proved the "separate but equal" clause lacking in providing educational opportunities to a Black school teacher who decided to pursue a graduate degree at the University of Oklahoma (Martin, 1998). These cases were crucial in establishing grounds regarding why "separate but equal" was not equal. Soon after, the 1954 landmark legislation, *Brown v. Board of Education* case, declared that apartheid schooling was unconstitutional. However, it is important to note that although this powerful piece of legislation destabilized school segregation, it did not end it and, in some cases, the mandate did little to change the systems of educational inequalities for African Americans. Martin (1998) elaborates:

> Thus, while *Brown* ended legalized Jim Crow in public school education, it did not end untold varieties of voluntary and actual racial segregation. Similarly, *Brown's* haphazard and varying nationwide implementation has not yielded the racially integrated elementary and secondary schools or equality of educational opportunity envisioned in the flush of its immediate afterglow. Likewise, in spite of federal mandates that the dual (separate white and black) college and university systems in various southern states be integrated, racially identifiable institutions persist: better-funded predominately white ones and less well-funded historically black colleges and universities. (p. 231)

In this passage, Martin (1998) explains that even with federal mandates to end racial segregation in schools, educational disparities continued. Charles Hamilton Houston and Thurgood Marshall are fitting to mention here for their contributions in dismantling the "separate but equal" doctrine (NAACP, n.d.). A decade later, the Civil Rights Act of 1964 outlawed discrimination against race, religion, and gender. Additionally, the Voting Rights Act of 1965 ended unequal voter registration requirements and racial segregation in schools and the workplace. Similarly, affirmative action policies and practices increased access to opportunities, particularly, admission policies that granted minorities entrance into PWIs. However, it could also be argued that these same policies placed more financial restrictions on HBCUs because these institutions now had to provide scholarships or tuition waivers to admit non-Black students. By 1969, the National Association for Equal Opportunity in Higher Education (NAFEO) was founded. This organization was established by HBCU presidents and serves as a national advocate for preserving, building, and sustaining HBCUs and predominately Black institutions (PBIs). Since its founding, NAFEO has served as a policy advocate for the 100 established HBCUs (Jackson, 2001; NAFEO, n.d.).

In the 1970s, college integration became more common because of the Civil Rights Movement and the Civil Rights Act of 1964. As a result, only 34% of Black students in college attended HBCUs. In 1980, President Jimmy Carter declared a federal initiative (Executive Order 12232) to help provide funding for HBCUs. However, in 1981, under the Ronald Reagan Administration, cutbacks in federal funds for education placed HBCUs in a state of financial peril. While the struggle for Black education was increasing, more African Americans were attending colleges and universities, and many more PWIs were admitting Black students, who were more or less their new consumers. However, racial barriers persisted. In 1992, *U.S. v. Fordice* found that even though public universities in Mississippi eliminated racially charged admissions policies that would deny African Americans from attending, the modest adjustment to these admission standards were still discriminatory, and continued to suppress the number of Black students who would be admitted. This court ruling helped to operationalize race-neutral admission practices at PWIs under the Equal Protection Clause of the 14th Amendment. However, the pendulum swung in both directions for admission policies. That is, as race-neutral practices at PWIs were expected to increase so an institution would not be subject to decreases in federal funding, HBCUs were also urged to increase their non-Black student enrollment or lose federal monies. Minor (2008) noted that Black colleges in Mississippi were deemed ineligible to receive funding because they failed to meet non-Black student enrollment quotas that were set by the state. With regards to public colleges and universities in the South, funding disparities similar to the Mississippi case was the norm.

Despite these educational challenges, Black students were persistent in their goal of pursuing higher education. In this regard, research indicates that African Americans generally maintain a strong interest in obtaining college and university degrees (Perna, 2000). National data on college enrollment reveals that the percentage of Black students in higher education has been steadily increasing since the late 1970s (NCES, 2012). In 1976, 10% of the overall college population was Black, and in 2011 this number increased to 15% (NCES, 2013). According to the U.S. Department of Education, in 2011, the total number of African Americans enrolled in U.S. accredited institutions was approximately three million (NCES, 2013), but only 9% of those students were enrolled in HBCUs, which accounted for 323,616 students. The remaining 91% of African American students were enrolled in public and private PWIs, two-year institutions, or non-degree granting schools (NCES, 2013). The increased enrollment among African Americans since the 1970s can be attributed to greater access and funding, as well as specific state-level racial integration measures that have increased the number of Black students who are attending PWIs.

Black students' decisions regarding which institutions to attend have been changing ever since the *Brown* case. With regards to HBCUs, the number of students enrolled has gradually increased since the late 1970s (mostly in public HBCUs), and most notably, national data highlights the growing number of non-Black students at these institutions (as illustrated in Table 1). In order to maintain funding and remain open, many public HBCUs have been forced to offer White students scholarships to attend. Table 1 reveals that enrollment for non-Black student populations since 1976 has increased to nearly 19% at HBCUs. In comparison, the Black student population at HBCUs has decreased from 85% to 81% respectively. This gradual trend demonstrates that while HBCU enrollment is on the rise, Black student populations at these institutions are decreasing.

When considering the gradual decline in the enrollment of Black students at HBCUs, some research points to federal legislation as a causal factor (Morrill, 2013; Perna et al., 2006). Because of the pernicious impact of legislation on HBCU attendance, Democratic U.S. Representative Mel Watt from North Carolina critiqued the federal loan policy changes made to the Parent Plus Loan in 2011. The policy revisions expanded the measuring criteria for a family's credit history and it created a decline in the number of students who could qualify. According to Watt (as cited by Morrill, 2013), during the 2013–2014 academic school year, only 27% of applicants at HBCUs were approved for Parent Plus Loans.

While Black student enrollment at HBCUs is declining, this is also the case at more selective postsecondary institutions. Selective PWIs still have very low levels of student diversity. Perna et al. (2006) used national data on postsecondary enrollment to examine attendance and completion of African Americans in southern states. They concluded that Black undergraduate enrollment in these states was more dependent upon institution type. For

Table 1. Fall enrollment at HBCUs (1976–2011)

Year	*Black population*	*Total population*	*% Non-Blacks*	*% Blacks*
1976	190,305	222,613	14.6	85.4
1980	190,989	233,557	18.3	81.7
1982	182,639	228,371	20.1	79.9
1984	180,803	227,519	20.6	79.4
1986	178,628	223,275	20.0	80.0
1988	194,151	239,755	19.1	80.9
1990	208,682	257,152	18.9	81.1
1991	218,366	269,335	19.0	81.0
1992	228,963	279,541	18.1	81.9
1993	231,198	282,856	18.3	81.7
1994	230,162	280,071	17.9	82.1
1995	229,418	278,725	17.7	82.3
1996	224,201	273,018	17.9	82.1
1997	222,331	269,167	17.5	82.5
1998	223,745	273,472	18.2	81.8
1999	226,592	274,321	17.4	82.6
2000	227,239	275,680	17.6	82.4
2001	238,638	289,985	17.8	82.2
2002	247,292	299,041	17.4	82.6
2003	253,257	306,727	17.5	82.5
2004	257,545	308,939	16.7	83.3
2005	256,584	311,768	17.8	82.2
2006	255,150	308,774	17.4	82.6
2007	253,415	306,515	17.4	82.6
2008	258,403	313,491	17.6	82.4
2009	264,090	322,789	18.2	81.8
2010	265,911	326,614	18.6	81.4
2011	263,414	323,616	18.9	81.1

Source: U.S. Department of Education, National Center for Education Statistics, Higher Education General Information Survey (HEGIS), "Fall Enrollment in Colleges and Universities," 1976 through 1985 surveys; Integrated Postsecondary Education Data System (IPEDS), "Fall Enrollment Survey" (IPEDS-EF:86–99); and IPEDS Spring 2001 through Spring 2012, Enrollment component. (This table was prepared January 2013.)

example, public flagship institutions showed the greatest disparities in diverse student enrollment and graduation rates, and were less responsive to mandates to desegregate public higher education. The researchers found that the greatest educational disparities in African American enrollment existed among the more selective institutions within the state (Perna et al., 2006). That is, for these particular colleges and universities, both student enrollment and graduation rates for African Americans were low. This research is particularly important because public flagship institutions have historically blocked African Americans from gaining access to educational opportunities.

HBCU MATRICULATION AND LIFE OUTCOMES OF GRADUATES

Despite shifting enrollment trends, HBCUs continue to award approximately 20% of the undergraduate degrees that African Americans receive (Thurgood Marshall College Fund, 2015; UNCF, 2014). While the number of African Americans attending PWIs is increasing, HBCUs still play an important role in Black higher education attainment (Albritton, 2012; Kim & Conrad, 2006; Thompson, 2008). During the 2009–2010 school year, approximately 31,000 bachelor's degrees were conferred at public and private HBCUs (Snyder & Dillow, 2012), and the following academic year, 33,000 bachelor's degrees were conferred by HBCUs (NCES, 2013). This speaks to the contemporary role of HBCUs as *titans of Black education*. Awokoya, Richards, and Myrick-Harris (2012) elaborate on the academic success and social mobility that HBCUs create for African Americans. They note:

> An analysis of the 2011 college rankings published by the *Washington Monthly* reveals that historically black colleges and universities (HBCUs) outperform many non-HBCUs, including some of the country's best known and prestigious institutions. (p. 3)

The U.S. Commission on Civil Rights (2010) reported on the educational effectiveness of HBCUs and confirmed many existing trends in the success of these institutions. The report indicates that students attending HBCUs were likely to engage in democratic societal practices that included charitable giving, and political and religious participation. They also had a greater propensity to major in the natural sciences (U.S. Commission on Civil Rights, 2010).

Additionally, Fleming (1984) found that African American males benefit greatly from attending HBCUs. This particular student demographic had the most social and academic gains during their years in an HBCU. Similarly, Warde (2008) conducted interviews with African American male HBCU graduates to determine the factors that positively contributed to their degree completion. Warde (2008) found that the most important factors were institutional support, as well as students' own realizations of the value of higher education. HBCUs also serve as an important contributor in promoting African Americans' participation in the science, technology, engineering, and mathematics (STEM) fields (Parks, 2003; Perna, 2001; Solorzano, 1995; Upton & Tanenbaum, 2014). Similarly, Perna et al. (2009) conducted a case study to identify institutional characteristics, policies, and practices that are attributed to the success and promotion of African American women in the STEM fields. Using Spelman College as an institutional model, findings derived from this study indicate the following: (a) students choose to attend Spelman because of its reputation for promoting women in the STEM fields; (b) students enter Spelman and maintain their educational and occupational goals and aspirations to persist to graduation; (c) Spelman College and its constituents acknowledge barriers that African American women face in the STEM fields; and (d) Spelman College attempts to counteract such barriers by providing support services, research opportunities, and cooperative learning environments for students (Perna et al., 2009). In this sense, the literature helps to support the fact that HBCUs are helping African Americans in some of the most difficult and competitive career fields (Upton & Tanenbaum, 2014). In spite of this success, the future of HBCUs is still in question. Thus, it is important to understand African American high school students' perceptions of HBCUs, since this is the population that is most likely to attend these schools. In the proceeding chapter, we report interview data from African American college-bound students regarding their thoughts about attending an HBCU.

CHAPTER 3

IN THEIR VOICE

High School Students' Perceptions about HBCUs

The African American high school students' narratives that are presented in this chapter are from a case study that explored students' perceptions about attending an HBCU. A case study is an investigation on a single unit, group, or entity in search of relationship meaning between a given context with aims to describe, explore, and explain real-life situations (Yin, 2009). The interviews were conducted between 2012 and 2013, and help to capture 21st century views on HBCUs. It is important to note that, similarly, in the *Dreamkeepers*, Ladson-Billings (1994) also conducted a case study to explore highly effective teachers in urban schools. And, Lipman (2004), in *High Stakes Education*, used a case study to explore school policies and practices in urban schools in Chicago. Case study design is recognized as being a rigorous qualitative research method.

Situated in a southeastern state, in this study we explored African American college-bound teens' perceptions on attending an HBCU. We placed flyers in public spaces and contacted school counselors regarding our investigation. Upon initial contact, more details, the recruitment script, and consent/assent forms were emailed or provided in person prior to collecting any data from the students (see *Appendix B*). Once consent from the parents and assent from the students were obtained, the prospective participants were asked to complete an information sheet, which identified them as African American and college-bound, meaning in the process of applying or have been accepted to attend a college or university (documentation was provided).

Two individual semi-structured interviews were conducted with 13 students who were enrolled in public high schools in a southeastern state (see *Appendix D* for the Interview Protocol). Pseudonyms were used for the students and the schools they attend. Most of these students were going to be the first generation of college-goers in their family. They were from working-class and middle-class backgrounds. The interviews were scheduled and conducted in public spaces that included: coffee shops, libraries, parks and shopping malls, as deemed appropriate and agreed upon by the participant and their parent/guardian. The interviews were conducted in neutral spaces where students were free from peer distractions and influence when answering questions. Eder and Fingerson (2003) assert: "In attempting to create a natural context for the interview, the researcher must also take care to avoid creating situations that remind youth of classroom lessons based on 'known-answer' questions" (p. 36).

In order to ensure internal validity of the research process, a few measures were put in place: (a) triangulation of the data; (b) member checks (meaning that the data was tested and confirmed by a member of the group from whom it was collected); (c) peer debriefing; and (d) an audit trail. First, triangulation of the data included the use of multiple sources of data throughout the data collection process. During the process, participants provided multiple sources of data to the researcher. This data served as confirmation of grade level, intentions to pursue higher education, and in some cases, confirmed plans after graduation. Additionally, multiple forms of data (audio recordings, memos, and reflexive notes) were collected to capture accurate depictions, responses, and perspectives of students. Second, member checks were conducted after each interview for each participant. Thematic coding was used to analyze and identify themes in the data. After the initial analysis of the combined interviews was conducted, a peer debriefing occurred to recount the researchers' attempts to describe and analyze the data. Additionally, each participant was given their interview transcript to review for accuracy.

PART I: PARTICIPANTS AND SCHOOLS

Table 2. Participants' demographic information

Name	*Gender*	*High school*
Jimmy	Male	Newsome H.S.
Tonya	Female	Newsome H.S.
Judy	Female	Madison H.S.
Troy	Male	Madison H.S.
Kenya	Female	Watts H.S.
Shane	Male	Arnold H.S.
Dorothy	Female	Arnold H.S.
Moesha	Female	Watts H.S.
Elise	Female	Arnold H.S.
Kim	Female	Newsome H.S.
Elisha	Male	Watts H.S.
Jenny	Female	Newsome H.S.
Mike	Male	Newsome H.S.

IN THEIR VOICE: WHAT IS AN HBCU?

To begin, it was important to understand how the participants defined an HBCU in their own voice. According to these college-bound students, HBCUs are defined and categorized as "historically Black," "majority Black," and an "environment for Black people." The participants shared that HBCUs were established primarily for the sake of educating African Americans. For example, Jimmy states, "Basically, the colleges that were around like back in the day were just for Black people really, like a lot of African Americans went." Dorothy extends this definition by stating: "Well, I think it's a school funded primarily for African Americans, but anybody can attend." According to the participants, HBCUs were created because African Americans were not allowed to attend other institutions due to legislation that restricted racial integration. Mike elaborates, "At an HBCU, it's just basically more of it was known for a historical reason, and it was founded for a historical reason, which has something to do with someone that was African American or Black, so to say." Since their inception, HBCUs have been viewed as institutions of higher education for African Americans. In this way, Shane notes:

> To me an HBCU is like, I don't want to say, I guess I always thought that HBCUs, they try to help Blacks get into college because not everywhere is going to accept a lot of Black students as an HBCU would.

Shane's comments relate to the importance of HBCUs in providing African Americans educational access. This point is expressed by all of our respondents.

The participants also recognize that HBCUs are majority Black schools. On the issue of what is an HBCU, Tonya shares, "My own definition would just be majority of the population is African American." Most of the participants equate the racial demographics of these institutions to their current and past role in serving African American students. Kenya recounts: "I would compare an HBCU–basically, to my whole life … because it's like I've been going to an HBCU all my life, HBCU elementary, middle, high school." Elisha added that HBCUs are: "Your average Black high school with more leeway."

Additionally, the participants felt that the HBCU was an environment for Black people. In this way, they provide an atmosphere that is fun, social, and accommodating for African American students. Moesha comments, "Environment. I think they're happy students, people that feel at home, like they're comfortable. I guess just having an environment where everyone can get to know about the history of Blacks." Dorothy adds: "I think of like a fun college experience … being around people that are just like you. Just everybody's the same I guess … like a family reunion." In this way, the participants also connect the Black college experience as one that is centered on developing a sense of community for its students. However, most of the students' knowledge about HBCUs did not come from school counselors, who in most cases had limited information or never mentioned these institutions, instead, they learned from family members, peers and the media, which also created some mis-conceptions about HBCUs.

The participants explained how lack of information about HBCUs may have influenced their perceptions about attending one. Shane recounts:

> I mean, it doesn't influence me one way or another, because at the end of the day, I have to make my own decision. But she (mom) should have told me, so I would be in the know. I don't like to research stuff, so she should have just told me. I wouldn't have to research. But it was fun, researching about it on my own. Now I can tell my kids about HBCUs.

Similarly, Tonya elaborates on her conversation with her mother regarding how she felt when various questions from the interviews were posed. She recounts:

> I told [my mom] I was coming to do an interview with you, and then she just asked me how it went and how I felt about it and I shared with her some of the stuff. Like I just said to you, how I found out that I didn't really know that much about HBCUs, and I felt like I wanted to do some more research on them, so I can just be more informed. I want to be one of those people who, like, know their school. Like, if someone's asking something about Hampton, I want to talk about it. I can give you the answer. Like I want to know my school's background, this, that, when it was founded. Like, I want to be that type of person that knows their school.

This issue of wanting to know more about HBCUs and being competent to answer questions about Black institutions is also shared by Moesha. She elaborates:

> I have those moments all the time. I feel like I can know more about certain things, about college. Some things, like I didn't know until you asked and then it made me want to know. I know more about how to access certain things and stuff.

Elise explains her miseducation about historical icons and their enrollment at HBCUs. She explains:

> America has shown that only white people can really go to college and everything. They have portrayed Martin Luther King, Coretta Scott–in a way, it has shown Martin Luther King really as a leader, and somebody that wanted to help people. You wouldn't really think he went to college and everything. I didn't ever know he would go to a black college.

Similarly, Jenny recounts how she will need to realign her miseducation about HBCUs with factual knowledge. She explains, "I do think that a lot of what I've been told may not necessarily be true, and that I have to do my own research before I believe stereotypes and ideals."

Connecting to this phenomenon about miseducation and lack of information about HBCUs, the participants reveal that the issue of counseling and advising in high school contributes to misconceptions about these institutions. Moesha explains: "The college advisor, Mrs. Stevens, she doesn't really say much about [HBCUs]." In addition, Shane shares: "They tell us about the different colleges, but they don't give a background story, like when we had a college fair, I think [N.C.] A&T was there." Similarly, Elise explains that her school provides a lot of information about colleges, but rarely does it pertain to HBCUs. She elaborates: "No, all I hear about is white colleges, really. It makes me feel sad that they won't show you can go to a black college, that it's the same education as going to a school like Appalachian State." Tonya elaborates:

> [My counselor] you know she'll say like "HBCUs stand for historically black colleges and universities," the population is you know predominately African American but, not really in detail. Maybe she just didn't want to be biased towards a certain type of institution. She is black, my guidance counselor, and her daughter actually goes to [Creek Ridge High School] and her daughter is going to A&T. I'm friends with her daughter. She's a senior, so I don't know. It's just a guess, maybe she doesn't want to be biased towards HBCUs, because her daughter is going to an HBCU, so she doesn't want to seem like she was rooting for HBCUs, or some people might want to go to predominantly white schools.

Jenny explains the lack of advisement and counseling about HBCUs in her high school: "Ms. Delmar's white, so she doesn't [talk about HBCUs]." Given these issues, there should be greater efforts made among high school counselors to provide students with accurate information about HBCUs.

IN THEIR VOICE: WHAT IS A PWI?

In addition to explaining what an HBCU is, the participants also defined a PWI. The participants suggested that PWIs are majority White institutions that are popular and commonly known. For example, Shane comments: "I think it's just like, White people going there, or you know like, majority of Caucasian people going to that school … it's a small percentage of other races." Jenny adds: "Isn't that colleges that are predominantly white and they scare all the minorities away?" According to the participants, PWIs primarily accommodate the racial needs of White students and while other ethnic groups are present at these institutions, African Americans are a minority.

The participants also characterize PWIs as commonly known or popular schools. Judy shares:

> Like [UNC Chapel Hill] and pretty much just the main schools everybody knows about, like … some people don't know like what [N.C. Central] is or where it is but if you say something like [Duke University] or [UNC Chapel Hill] they'll know like exactly where it is and, what their mascot is, 'cause like, they're mostly seen on like, television for like, their basketball or anything else they have.

Similarly, when commenting on what a PWI is, Elisha adds:

> They get more exposure because a PWI, they get the chance to play on TV and ESPN and stuff, and you also have [HBCUs], who goes to the championship every year, and they don't get to play on TV until they go to the championship, but you've got the PWIs still losing real bad and they get their game on TV every day.

Elisha comments on the lack of visibility and exposure that HBCUs generally receive.

IN THEIR VOICE: INSTITUTIONAL DIFFERENCES BETWEEN HBCUS AND PWIS

The participants also shared their perspectives on the institutional differences between HBCUs and PWIs. First, the participants comment that in terms of admission standards, they believe PWIs are more selective and therefore are elite institutions. Jenny notes that, "Admission standards, it seems like predominately White colleges are harder to get into, a lot harder to get into." Similarly, when identifying how these institutions are perceived, Mike adds:

> You can't get into PWIs, because you're not white to uphold that standard, of getting a 4.0 plus … you have to have more extra-curricular activities, a better GPA, a better SAT score, a better ACT score. The way I see it is you have a bigger plate to stand up to, because a lot of these IB kids are coming out with 4.8s, 4.7s.

Kenya also comments:

> To me, I feel like the predominately white schools have higher standards, like higher GPAs, higher grades for classes, higher everything … I feel like their standards are not as high, even though African Americans can have high standards. But I just feel like [HBCUs are] just not that high.

Kenya's comments, along with Jenny and Mike, may be connected to the negative portrayals or the underlying assumption that Black colleges have automatic acceptance policies, which some schools may, but that is not the case for all HBCUs.

Next, students share that they feel that HBCUs are more relaxed and social. In this way, HBCU campuses provide students with greater opportunities to engage in campus activities, to bond with colleagues, and interact with other students. Troy recounts:

> At a PWI I feel like the only time that everyone is social with each other is at a social event such as basketball games, football games, umm, something has to be happening. While at a HBCU, nothing has to be happening at all for everyone to come together and do something. I've seen where they're all meeting and there's like and, I don't know, like, every HBCU I've been to there's like this room with like pool tables and all this other stuff. And it's always packed with black people; I'm like okay I can get use to this. They're all just hanging out, like they probably just met but, it's just that family, they come together. There's a family difference.

Kim adds: "I think HBCUs are a little bit tighter-knit. Like, everybody feels like they're more connected to each other, like more a little family than predominantly white schools." This perspective is also shared by Tonya who elaborates that:

> I just feel like the, the atmosphere, would just be different. Like, I don't want to say this is like a biased way but I don't know, I just feel like black people are just more like you know laid back, there are some really you know like strict, not saying I'm not going to be on like top

> of my work or anything, but like, just kind of laid back. I feel like predominately white institutions are more like strict, uptight on your work … I guess how people think that black people are just loud, or how they may interact with their friends and like you know just try and party and be all crazy or people are always like you know, every time black people get to the party stuff always gets you know messed up or shut down or gets crazy. Versus at PWIs I guess, they just know how to act and behave. And they're not going to get crazy and the cops aren't going to get called.

In sum, according to participants, HBCUs and PWIs display vast differences both academically and socially. In their view, PWIs are associated with catering to White students and being highly selective and academically rigorous, whereas HBCUs are defined as predominantly Black environments that are more socially accommodating to students. It should be noted that the participants' HBCU and PWI definitions and perceptions about institutional differences are based on interrelated issues. Some of the participants were speaking first-hand from visiting various institutions and experiencing the environment, and for others the media and popular culture played a crucial role.

What the Media Tells Me about Black Colleges

For the participants, the role of the media also influences their perceptions about Black institutions of higher education. The participants explain how movies, social media and news reporting affirm both positive and negative things they have heard about HBCUs. Most commonly referenced, the participants discussed how *Drumline*, a film produced in 2002 that featured a college freshman's entrance into the marching band and his experiences adjusting to college life, influenced their views on the Black college experience. Kim elaborates on watching *Drumline* and wanting to have a similar college experience because of the positive light in which the Black college was showcased. She comments:

> I knew it was about [N.C.] A&T, but I know there's different A&Ts all across the country. That made me want to go to A&T right there. That's the real reason I want to go to A&T, because of that movie. I don't know, it just really promoted a black school, like there was nothing wrong with that school, everything was good. It was really positive. There wasn't anything bad about it. They also had a [White student]. He

> got a minority scholarship, because he was a white person on the band, at A&T, but he went there because he lived down the street. It was just a really positive movie.

Shane adds that while he was very young when he first saw the movie, *Drumline* still influenced his thinking about the Black college experience. He recounts:

> When I saw that movie I was like "they look like they having fun." They love it there; they love it at that campus. So I mean, I guess the thought did cross my mind there but I didn't, I didn't really think about it because when I saw that movie I was like I don't know, 4th or 5th grade? No it couldn't have come out in 4th or 5th grade, I don't know. I was young so I wasn't really thinking about college, but I mean I was like "Oh, they look like they having fun." And I asked my mom "what college was that?" she was like "oh, it's A&T."

Similarly, Moesha discusses how the movie *Drumline* helped her to see the Black college social environment and how students bond together. She shares:

> I guess it gives somewhat of a black experience of an HBCU. Because it shows all how they hang out, how all the black kids hang out together, and what they may do in certain situations, and how they might bond, socially and stuff. I actually liked the whole movie, but I think I liked how the band worked together, in a family-type way, everybody became cool.

Another movie that was frequently discussed among the participants was *Stomp the Yard*. This film was released in 2007 and shadows an entering freshman's journey through pledging in a fraternity. The movie centers on the rhythmic, artistic, group movements of stepping as a major aspect in Black Greek-letter organizations, which are popularized at HBCUs. Jimmy shares that the movie helped him to debunk early perceptions that HBCUs were "ghetto," because the movie captured "the culture" of a Black college. He adds:

> I see how colleges are, I see how fraternities are and I'm not ready to go for fraternities but it's actually, it's the culture it's the culture I can relate to and it would be more easier to adjust to. They definitely portrayed it more better than I thought they would because usually, usually it wasn't too ghetto, because that's what friends have told me.

Similarly, Elise provides insight on how one scene in the movie was extremely influential for her because it showed African American historical figures who had attended and graduated from an HBCU.

> You learn–when he went inside the–I don't know what it's called, but when he went inside where all the Greeks are at, and he saw Coretta Scott and Rosa Parks, when he saw all that, I was like, "Wow, all these people went to a black college." I never would have known that. I didn't know they went to college and stuff, and just seeing it was a black college, it was like, "Oh." They didn't make it like it's ghetto, shooting, fighting and all of that. It didn't make you feel, if you went to a black college, I have to watch my back.

Jimmy and Elise are both able to reconstruct their views on what a Black college experience is as it relates to the movie's depictions of HBCUs. However, there are instances in which the media presents Black colleges in an undesirable light and, according to students, this further reinforces negative perceptions. Tonya elaborates on how people on social media such as Twitter and Facebook, depict Black colleges as party schools. She shares:

> I think there was an incident with partying or something like that, and some girl might have gotten really drunk and her picture was, like, surfacing, I guess, on the internet. So that's a negative thing, but on the positive side, a lot of them are doing well in college and are on the Dean's list or something, so they promote that on Twitter as well. It doesn't, like, change the way I feel about them, but it does kind of just make me take a second look at it, like why does everybody have something so negative to say about it, because then again, I don't really let it phase me, because it's kind of like people on the outside, looking in. They're not there every day, going to school there. They don't know what it's like. That could just be a one bad day at that school, and it's just made public. You don't know the everyday life of the school. You're just an outsider, looking in. Everybody can't base their judgment just off of that, when they don't really know what's going on. I don't really let it affect me. I mean, I don't think every institution is perfect, but I don't like how some of the media just … I don't like how they just target it to, I guess, HBCUs, because the same thing could be going on at a predominantly white institution that might not just be blown as big, just because they're not black, they're white.

Tonya recognizes how HBCUs are type-casted as party schools and places where social deviance occurs, but if the same behaviors were to occur at a PWI, media attention would be minimized. Troy adds to this sentiment when recalling what he learned from the news in regards to a hazing incident at a major southeastern university. Troy explains:

> All I've heard really is with FAMU and their band and the hazing. Like I said before, they're not going to get all the credit they can. [UNC Chapel Hill] does this; great. [University of South Carolina] does this; great. [North Carolina State University], they've got this much money so that they could try and find a cure for this; great. But HBCUs, the first thing that happens–and HBCUs do the exact same thing. They get funding for this and that, but the only thing you're really going to hear is, "Oh, they got in trouble for hazing. This person died." Well, it happens every year at a lot of PWIs, and you will never hear about it.

Dorothy adds that these negative perceptions conveyed through the media, shaped her parents' thinking about the Black college experience, and whether they wanted her to attend an HBCU. She elaborates:

> I heard about the lockdown at A&T. I think they thought the guy had a rifle, but he had an umbrella with a strap. I remember my mom texted me, and she was like, "You still want to go to A&T?"

In sum, the majority of the participants perceive the Black college experience to be an environment in which they can relate to their peers because they share the same culture. Additionally, since there is a shared culture among students, the participants felt that the Black college experience is also about getting an education and working hard, as well as having the freedom to grow into a more mature person. Visits to HBCU campuses have helped some of the participants to reaffirm and dispel existing notions surrounding what a Black college can offer them academically, socially, and culturally. Movies, social media, and news also play an important role in how students perceive a Black College experience. Similar to campus visits, the media can serve as a pendulum for guiding perceptions about HBCUs; students can either perceive the experience as culturally invigorating, a place to learn, and personable, or they can see the institutions as stereotypical party schools in undesirable, dangerous locations. However, the main question that buttressed our investigation was: *What are Black high school students' perceptions about attending an HBCU?*

When asked about their viewpoints regarding attending an HBCU, the participants explained that these institutions were "a good choice" for Black students. Shane comments:

> I think that most people should attend a HBCU. Well, most black people … I think that for me, and my opinion, I think HBCUs are a good choice, first choice, in my opinion. They help you get into college where places might not accept you. I think that they're a-okay with me.

Mike elaborates that HBCUs build upon one's cultural identity which, in his opinion, is vital. Mike explains:

> You're missing out if you don't attend. I think you're open to more options because they take one thing that you have in common, which is blackness, and then they build upon that.

Troy shares that HBCUs should be experienced by Black and White students to help both demographics understand cultural differences that exist among both groups. He elaborates:

> I think it's a great thing. I think, most black students should do it, some white. I think all, I think they all should. I feel like that's an experience all black students should do, be their area primarily, I mean of majority white, go to majority black… to see if there's a difference … culturally.

Troy suggests that Black and White students should attend HBCUs so that they can learn more about each other's culture. Overall, the participants postulate that they perceive an HBCU to be a good choice for Black students to attend.

Learn More about African American History and Culture

Additionally, some of the students also connected their perceptions about HBCUs to learning more about African American history and culture. Even though Kim will not be attending an HBCU, she explains that she would be privy to African American history if she were to attend one of these institutions. She comments:

> I would learn more about the history. It's a lot of unknown history that we didn't know about in the black community. When I was at Arnold H.S., we had an African American cultural class. It was taught in a class, and it was a class about African Americans. I feel like, at an HBCU, they would have more of those than at a predominately white college.

Similarly, Troy elaborates on one of his visits to an HBCU. Through his trip, he discovered much about historical figures who had attended the college. He shares:

> Everywhere you go at an HBCU they have dates here and there and eventually you learn them by heart. For instance, at [Morehouse College] they have a huge Martin Luther King statue, simply because he went to that school. And they have a museum on campus of every person who has contributed to the college. White and black, and you learn about the history of it. And it's just they teach you a whole lot more, about you.

Moesha adds to Troy's comments about HBCUs' historical value by noting the museums and information about African Americans that is provided by these institutions. She states:

> Because you might have some history around the campus that might be placed in different areas, like the museums around it or something, that you could learn yourself, that you could learn about historically black people and stuff like that, instead of going to a white college. They tend to have information about African Americans and you can't really–I'm not sure how to explain it. I don't know. It would be different, because having it come from someone else, that's not of the same race, it would sound different, I would say.

Shane also reflects on his visit to an HBCU. He shares how the history of the institution influences him:

> A&T had so much history in itself. Like the lunch counter sit in … I think that they can teach you about like, thriving and going the extra step and all that courage and stuff.

The participants also share that HBCUs provide an enhanced cultural experience for students. Jenny explains that attending one of these institutions would make her feel great pride about her culture. She elaborates:

> I'd like to be able to say I went to an HBCU. I think saying that kind of–part of it is like I'm saying I'm proud of my race and my heritage, and I'm going to a place where it was historically people like me. Yeah, it's still a college and everything, but it's also got that extra with it.

Similarly, Shane explains that there are positive aspects of attending an HBCU that are related to developing greater cultural awareness. He explains:

> I think every, I mean I don't think that everybody should but, I think that, for the people who are so stuck on like culture and like "Oh, I want to learn more about black culture," go to the HBCU. That's where to get the black culture, they will know where you been. They don't, like a … NC State don't know where you been, there might be white teachers there, you don't know, they don't know our life, they don't know what we been through.

Similarly, Moesha discusses how HBCUs help students to get to know their history through hosting social and cultural events. Moesha explains:

> I think that it'll be a good experience, honestly. I think that, like I said at the beginning, you get to know more of what your culture is, and how other people act, I guess, and just trying to get to–I don't know, I guess just trying to get to know different people that you may clique with, or I may clique with, whatever.

The participants posit that HBCU environments provide them with opportunities to learn more about African American history and culture. In this way, HBCUs provide cultural capital (cultural knowledge regarding the rules of engagement in society) to their students.

Better Academic Performance

As a related school culture issue, some participants mention how HBCUs could provide them with better academic support systems than PWIs. Troy elaborates:

> Classrooms are smaller, teach, I mean. There are large classes. Howard is huge, FAMU is the biggest HBCU in the nation, but the classes are a lot smaller and you would get 1 on 1, they know you by name. While at PWI you may be number 346.

Similarly, Tonya adds that the HBCU learning environment is less intimidating for her because she feels like everyone is "on the same level." She shares:

> In my opinion sometimes I feel like, for instance like even now in high school I feel like, I'm not intimidated by you know people of other races, but if it's like me and like a white girl in my class, I don't know just feel like she might do better on the test or something. I don't know, but if it's just black people I just feel like we're all equal, we're all on the same level, we're just all the same, you know.

Next, Kenya discusses how she perceives that the learning environments at HBCUs are more supportive to a student's emotional needs and in doing so, she would feel more academic support in these institutions. She comments:

> Because I feel like–I'm very laid back. People tell me I'm too laid back, but if I get pushed too hard, I'm going to quit. Like, I don't mean to, but some things I cannot handle. I'm very emotional, and I know if I go to a school where I'm being pushed too hard, I'm going to start crying and I'm going to go home. I will not finish if I'm too emotional to handle that. I didn't want to go to a predominantly white school because I know it's going to be too challenging for me, and I'm probably going to drop out.

However, one participant reveals that even though HBCUs would be good for Black students, they should not feel obligated to attend; "to each his own." Dorothy elaborates: "I think to each his own. Like, if that's where you want to go, that's where you go. But if you don't, you don't."

A Sense of Pride in Graduating from an HBCU

In addition to believing that HBCUs were a good choice for Black students, the participants also felt that there was a sense of pride in graduating from HBCUs. For example, Troy explains:

> I would be extremely proud of myself if that's what you're asking. Like, what would I think of myself? I would think that's a great achievement 'cause HBCUs are, I mean they may be looked down upon my white people but they are no joke. So, say I got my degree from here or there. It's still something to be extremely proud of.

Jenny shares her thoughts on graduating from an HBCU in relation to her prior educational experiences. She comments:

> To me, it's kind of like there's power in numbers. If you come–I would feel good coming from a school that is historically black, because I had such a bad experience in a school that was historically white, and I was one of only two black kids there, so it would mean a lot to me to go to a school that is–used to be, at least–for black people. I don't know, I just think it's a little more sentimental than going to just a regular university, like [North Carolina State University]. If I didn't go to an HBCU I don't think I would feel as proud. I would still feel proud if I got my bachelor's degree and I got this and whatever, but I think going to an

> HBCU is definitely something sentimental to me, and it's kind of more embracing myself and my people more.

Similar to Jenny, Moesha also elaborates that while she will be happy to graduate from any college or university, she would feel an added sense of accomplishment if she completed her degree at an HBCU because of the historical importance these institutions hold. She shares:

> I'd probably feel accomplished, for one, because you've made it through four years of college. I mean, who wouldn't feel accomplished? Like, I feel–yeah, I'd just say accomplished … Yeah, I got the experience to go through it and actually experience four years of being with people in an HBCU and the history and background and stuff about that campus.

Mike sums it up by stating, "I'd be stronger for graduating from an HBCU." In this way, he feels like the HBCU has more to offer him not only in regards to his academic self, but also in personal development.

Additionally, some of the participants who had a family member who attended an HBCU, placed greater emphasis on the importance of graduating from a Black postsecondary institution. Moesha shares:

> I mean, [my dad] would probably be like, "Yeah, you're accomplishing," you've got the experience of a historically Black college and stuff like that, but I think he'd be proud.

Similarly, Kim relays how meaningful it would be to her family if she graduated from an HBCU. She states:

> I think it's important to my family, my grandmother was the only one who went to an HBCU out of my family. I think it's important to her because she always pushes me to go to Johnson C. Smith. She just wants me to go to a black college. She doesn't know anything about Greensboro. You know, they don't really talk about those colleges among the black community, so she just wants me to go to a black college, because that's what she knows. She went to college in the 60s or the 70s, and it was hard to get into a white school back in those days, so now she's like, "Go to a black college. That's where you're going to fit in best at, so just go there."

On the other hand, some students expressed indifference about graduating from an HBCU. They explain that the mere fact of graduating is a sense of accomplishment that they will have regardless of the institution. Dorothy expresses that where she attends school is not important to her, but completing a degree is the most important thing. In this sense, she does not feel like it matters if one graduates from an HBCU. Dorothy explains:

> I mean, I would be proud of myself for graduating from anywhere, but I think I would be–well, I would look at what did I accomplish when I was there, and then, if I didn't accomplish something that I had wanted to, then I'd probably be upset with myself, but if I accomplished everything that I thought that I would in college, then it wouldn't matter, because I still did community service or whatever, that I want to do in college. It wouldn't matter where I am, just as long as I accomplish those goals that I want to.

This indifference about HBCUs is also shared by Kim who comments: "[I would feel] that I'm smart, just for graduating college," and Jimmy who recounts: "It doesn't really matter to me, as long as I get my education."

Job Opportunities Are Questionable with HBCU Degrees

In addition to the notion of HBCUs being party schools, many of the participants were concerned about the currency of an HBCU degree in the workforce. Tonya explains the concerns she has about obtaining an HBCU degree. She comments:

> Some people may look down upon HBCUs, and that could, like, hinder some job opportunities, because some employers may still have not accepted the fact, you know, or still not, like, fully open to everybody being equal. I don't know. So, they might look down upon someone going to an HBCU, so it could affect some job opportunities in the future.

Similarly, Elise adds that when compared to a degree from a PWI, an HBCU degree has less value. Elise states, "In terms of getting a job, the education. They're going to treat [graduates of PWIs] better." Kim provides a scenario in which she examines how her degree from an HBCU would compare to one from a PWI. She elaborates:

> Like, my manager I have now, it's two hostesses, me and this other girl named Porscha. If Porscha went to [UNC Chapel Hill] and I went to A&T and we both came back and applied for a job as the financial director or something like that, I feel like she would get the job because she went to [UNC Chapel Hill]. My boss, he'd be like–okay, you know, you have the same degree, you know you graduated with honors, but I feel like he wouldn't give me the same opportunity as he gave her.

Similarly, Judy explains the perceptions regarding HBCU graduates in the workplace. She explains:

> Like, I guess they would have like, different like, bias against like, a black institution like somewhere like [Fayetteville State University] or something like that they might think like, she's like, ghetto or something like that, especially if I work for like an all-white company or something like that, then they might do that but I don't know about everybody they might not be like a person to judge off of something like that but, if they are, then maybe they'd be something like that. Or if I went to a white school, and I worked at a black company, they might think like I'm super smart or something like that or really educated.

Elisha shares a conversation he had with his parents about attending an HBCU versus a PWI, and the anticipated outcomes of both institutions. Elisha comments:

> When I got accepted to [Yale University], my parents really wanted me to go there, and when I told them I wanted to go to [Winston Salem], they were like, "Why are you picking [Winston State] over [Yale University]?" I was like, "I always wanted to go to an HBCU." They said, "But you got this opportunity to go to [Yale University] and your life will be pretty much set after going there." I said, "My life will pretty much be set after going to [Winston Salem], too." After I said that, they said, "Well, you know what you want to do, so pursue your dreams."

Similar to Elisha, Kenya weighs her educational options. Interestingly, Kenya argues that while credentials from PWIs may seem superior to HBCU degrees, she adds that the type of HBCU should be taken into consideration. She explains:

> I feel like, if it's an ivy league HBCU, they would think higher of me. Like a known HBCU, something they know about, not like one of those schools like Johnson C. Smith University, maybe. A lot of people don't know about that. They know about Spelman, things like that. They know about A&T.

Dorothy shares the same sentiment. She asserts that the type of HBCU could be more telling of success after graduation. She elaborates:

> I think if it was a like a historical black college I graduated from, I think they would look at the quality of the school. Maybe. I know like

sometimes people are like, if you graduate from like Morehouse or Howard or something, like "oh, you went to like that type of HBCU." And then like the other ones are classified as "oh, that type." So I think it would depend on the school maybe.

Both Kenya and Dorothy's comments allude to the ways in which HBCUs are ranked among colleges (this will be discussed in the final chapter). In this way, according to students, some HBCUs are seen as having standards that are equal to PWIs. The students expressed great concerns about how HBCUs are ranked, whether they are accredited, and ultimately, whether they can get a job with these degrees. Elisha comments: "Money is the main thing. Because the more money I get on scholarship, the less that has to come out of my pocket." Jimmy adds, "… how much the money, the school will be able to give me to go to school, like financial aid." Similar to Elisha and Jimmy, Dorothy shares that a scholarship can greatly influence one's decision on which school to attend. She comments: "When I got the scholarship from Queens, I was like, I'm done." Tonya considers the overall cost of tuition and the financial aid she will receive. She elaborates: "I'm still liking Hampton, because I also have a scholarship there. I have to just look at all my acceptances, but then NC State is in-state, so then it also might be cheaper." In this way, Tonya considers in-state colleges as being more financially viable for her education.

Additionally, the reputation of the institution is also a significant factor in the general consideration of which college to attend. Kim shares how she looks at the reputation of the program within her field of study. She remarks: "It has to be on the list of the best schools in America … Elon University, I know they have a great law program." Elise adds to this perspective when considering which college she will transfer to after completing her studies at a community college: "Maybe Winston Salem. I heard it was a really good school." Dorothy considers the reputations of HBCUs in comparison to PWIs with regards to the prospect of being accepted into a graduate school. She elaborates:

> Like myself, I, I looked into it and I thought about it but, I didn't know, like if I had gone to a black school and then graduated, would people have looked at me differently? Would I have been looked down on? Like if I say like I went to maybe Johnson C. Smith University or something, and then I tried to go to medical school, you know. Would I get denied because I went to a historical Black college? So that's something I had

> to look at and consider, and that's why I didn't apply to one … [I chose Queens] especially because of the program I wanted to go into but also because I would be use to the school.

In addition to the financial aid package and overall reputation of the institution, the students questioned if they would get jobs if they attended HBCUs. The students liked the fact that HBCUs were more communal and supportive, but they had to weigh their options more deeply. Additionally, students understood the role that HBCUs played historically, and while they felt that they were "a good choice," they were most likely to attend a school with a strong reputation that would provide them with funding, and where they could earn their degrees and obtain a job. In the final chapter, we discuss our findings in relation to other research and we provide policy recommendations.

CHAPTER 4

WHERE ARE THE BLACK TITANS AND WHAT CAN THEY LEARN FROM PROSPECTIVE STUDENTS?

HBCUs: INSTITUTIONAL FACTORS

The interviewees in our study expressed an understanding regarding the role that HBCUs play in the education of African Americans. In fact, when asked about their viewpoints regarding attending an HBCU, some of the students explained that these institutions were "a good choice" for Black students. As noted, Shane comments:

> I think that most people should attend an HBCU. Well, most black people … I think that for me, and my opinion, I think HBCUs are a good choice, first choice, in my opinion. They help you get into college where places might not accept you. I think that they're okay with me.

Similarly, Mike elaborates that HBCUs build upon one's cultural identity which, in his opinion, is vital. Mike explains:

> You're missing out if you don't attend. I think you're open to more options because they take one thing that you have in common, which is blackness, and then they build upon that.

Troy shares that Black and White students should experience HBCUs to help both groups share and learn from each other. He elaborates:

> I think it's a great thing. I think, most black students should do it, some white. I think all, I think they all should. I feel like that's an experience all black students should do, be their area primarily [meaning if they are Black or White], I mean of majority white, go to majority black … to see if there's a difference … culturally.

This finding contrasts with Freeman's study (1999), who found that African American students who attended predominately Black high schools were more likely to want to attend a PWI. Although the culture and supportive environment of HBCUs was not going to be the decisive factor in terms of which college or university our interviewees attended, in general, they perceived these institutions as being "a good choice" for Black students.

Similarly, other studies suggest that HBCUs serve as a mecca of cultural capital and identity development (Cokley & Chapman, 2008; Davis, 1998; Fleming, 1984; Franklin & Savage, 2004). Chavous et al. (2002) and Dillon (1999) found that students with strong racial identities exhibited higher academic performance. However, students who felt racial and cultural incongruence had lower academic performance (Chavous, Rivas, Green, & Helaire, 2002). Additionally, Outcalt and Skewes-Cox (2002) found that students at HBCUs demonstrated higher levels of academic involvement than their Black counterparts at PWIs. That is, more students reported completing their work on time, tutoring other students, completing extra class work, and did not feel bored in class. Perhaps telling of the overall climate and racially supportive environment at HBCUs, the researchers found that "fewer HBCU students tend to attend racial/cultural workshops, take ethnic courses, or belong to racial/cultural organizations than PWI students" (Outcalt & Skewes-Cox, 2002, p. 338). Since these cultural outlets are more or less built into HBCUs, students felt less of a need to sign up for a specific cultural organization or support group, which is a more common practice for minority students attending PWIs.

With regards to overall satisfaction with their institutions, Outcalt and Skewes-Cox (2002) found that 80% of students reported being "satisfied" or "very satisfied" with their experiences at HBCUs, while 74% of Black students attending PWIs said that they were "satisfied" or "very satisfied." The authors explain:

> African American students at HBCUs tended to be more satisfied with the sense of community, student-to-student interaction, and the availability of leadership opportunities than their counterparts at comparable PWIs. (Outcalt & Skewes-Cox, 2002, p. 342)

Similarly, Thompson (2008) explored the unique academic and supportive environment that HBCUs provide to students. The author also notes that HBCU graduates typically go on to complete a graduate degree, and even doctoral training. Additionally, Albritton (2012) notes:

> Whether they are first generation college students or the sons and daughters of college-educated parents, Black students who attend HBCUs benefit from a strong and committed network of faculty, staff, and professional leaders who seek to offer learning opportunities that will increase possibilities for long-term success. (p. 327)

In addition to the support systems that HBCUs provide, research has also indicated that there are strong peer and faculty interactions at HBCUs, which contributes to student achievement. Fountaine (2012) investigated the student-faculty interactions at HBCUs with regards to the experiences of female doctoral students. The findings revealed that strong student-faculty relationships are nurtured at HBCUs, which contributes to higher graduation rates. Since research suggests that HBCUs are indeed more supportive in terms of African Americans' academic and social development, this may explain why they generally excel at these institutions.

Students who attend HBCUs look to these schools to help reinforce their cultural identities and provide them with an experience that PWIs currently do not offer them. This relates to Obenga (1992) and Clarke's (1977) treaties on the communal, and cultural and intellectual traditions of pre-colonial Africans, as well as the cultural retentions and heritage that remains with African Americans. This communal legacy, which crossed over the Atlantic Ocean, continues to permeate Black institutions of higher learning. For example, as noted in the case of the first university in the world, the University of Waset, also called the Grand Lodge of Luxor, there was a tradition of education that Europeans came to admire and learn from (Diop, 1974). The Greek Historian Plutarch, who wrote the book *Parallel Lives,* provides biographies where he explains that Thales, Plato, and Pythagoras all came to Egypt/Kemet and studied and consulted with the teachers and priests (as cited by Scardigli, 1995). Nevertheless, while the communal aspects of African traditions are present at HBCUs, since most of today's Black colleges and universities are modeled after White schools as Anderson (1988) notes, specific knowledge and curricula focusing on Africa hardly enters these institutions. As a result, the information about pre-colonial Africa and its continuity to the African American experience is minimally reflected in the curriculum in Black schools, which may challenge these institutions to become more culturally relevant with regards to pre-colonial African educational traditions.

In the scope of our study, it is important to note that the participants connected more with the social and cultural aspects of HBCUs, as influenced by the mainstream media, their friends, and family, rather than information provided by these institutions. Perhaps this further supports the notion that prospective (and current) students would benefit from greater institutional knowledge about HBCUs and the heritage of continental Africa, and Africans in education (Du Bois, 1903; Means-Coleman, 2002; Sun, Cooks, Rinehart, & Williams, 2002).

RACIAL AWARENESS

Regarding the Black college experience, the students in our study had a general sense of race consciousness in knowing that HBCUs were created for African Americans (Bell, 1992; Clarke, 1977; Gray, 2001). Since U.S. race relations continues to be tumultuous, especially in light of recent police shootings and the killing of young Black males, i.e. Jordan Davis, Jonathan Ferrell, Michael Brown, and Trayvon Martin slayings (which are reminiscent of the lynching of Black men), where in each case the aggressor was exonerated, which created racial protest across the nation; our participants had a general sense that there were schools that were created for Blacks (HBCUs), and ones that were created for Whites (PWIs). Although most of these students are far removed from the Civil Rights period of the 1960s and 1970s and school desegregation, the resegregation of America's public schools is an issue that they may certainly be familiar with.

In particular, students expressed how district rezoning, student demographics, and school resources were different within the same district. In addition, they explained that generally, predominately Black schools were in poor neighborhoods and predominately White schools were in nicer, richer parts of the city. Students were not oblivious to the educational inequalities that existed within their own schooling experiences. Their assertions are supported by literature that elaborates on structural inequities in public schools (Bell, 1992; Darling-Hammond, 2010; Kozol, 2005; Parker, 1998; Schwitzer et al., 1999). Many of our participants attended either majority Black high schools or in some cases, majority White high schools, and so this may have made an impression on them that indeed, HBCUs *are* for Black students.

In PWIs, many African Americans still complain that they experience marginalization and limited academic support. These experiences with marginalization also contribute to Black students social adjustment or maladjustment when engaging in the mainstream culture of PWIs. Relatedly, Black students' racial identity and social development is one issue in public K-12 education that impacts higher education. Woodson (1933) notes, "the thought of inferiority of the Negro is drilled into him in almost every class he enters and in almost every book he studies" (p. 1). This issue might still be true in spite of all that has occurred to provide equal access and opportunities to African Americans in public K-12 schools and perhaps in PWIs as well. In public schools, Blacks students are forced to operate in—and understand the "culture of power" (Delpit, 1995), which more or less operationalizes White cultural ethos as the norm for the classroom, and concurrently, normalizes the behaviors and expectations for the workplace and the occupational ladder. In K-12 public schools and PWIs, minority students are forced to master the ethos, as well as the codes and rules that are related to the dominant group. Thus, in schools, minority students are often silenced or othered in the classroom (Delpit, 1988, 1995). When students are marginalized in schools, they often have poor academic performance and become disengaged. This speaks to the strength of HBCUs, because they are able to place Black students in a social and cultural embryonic environment that is nurturing, while also preparing them to operate in predominately White spaces. Therefore, the students thrive. This is something that PWIs struggle to achieve.

In this sense, Douglas (1998) noted that first-year African American students felt disconnected on their campus due to limited services and activities that were available to them. Additionally, Schwitzer, Griffin, Ancis, and Thomas (1999) investigated 4th year African American college students' social adjustment experiences at PWIs and found that students felt vastly underrepresented among the student population. Students also mentioned receiving less support throughout their collegiate experience and having difficulty transitioning into college life.

In PWI settings, research reveals that Black students have a limited amount of interactions with faculty (Schwitzer, Griffin, Ancis, & Thomas, 1999). In the Schwitzer et al. study (1999), the participants expressed that they were less likely to receive classroom support, academic advising, or career guidance because of feelings of intimidation due to racism and negative perceptions of Black students at PWIs. This finding is echoed by a study conducted by Fries-Britt and Turner (2002) in which Black students at PWIs experienced a lack of interaction with White faculty and peers, and described many campus activities as being aimed towards White students. Rist (1970, 2000) explained how structural inequalities and teacher perceptions of Black students contributes negatively to student achievement.

Additionally, Wallace and Bell (1999) reported that students felt pressure to assimilate while attending a PWI. They found that Black students attending PWIs engaged in mainstream culture, school activities, and social events as a means of enhancing their collegiate experience, as well as to make them feel like less of a social-outlier. Being bi-cultural or having exposure to different cultural and social groups can most certainly be an asset to students. Fries-Britt and Turner (2002) explain that Black students who enroll at PWIs have often interacted more with the dominant group and may share many existing, associated behaviors. They explain:

> To survive on White campuses, some Black students consciously assimilate into the White culture, but this does not mean that they know less about Black culture. More than likely, Black students at TWIs [Traditionally White Institutions] have learned to become bicultural, developing a repertoire of expressions and behaviors from both the White and Black community and switching between them as appropriate. (Fries-Britt & Turner, 2002, p. 320)

While there are benefits associated with attending a PWI, race relations can make the experience difficult and painful for Black students. Institutional racism and structural inequalities in schooling are still pervasive, and greatly affect the achievement and life outcomes of African American students. Schwitzer et al. (1999) found that students felt elements of institutional racism in college. In particular, students mentioned that their university condoned separatist mainstream White activities with regards to social clubs and events. This finding is also consistent with Douglas' (1998) study which concluded that students felt voluntary racial separation on their campus. That is, students felt isolated in popularized campus-wide events and activities and as a result, formed networks with other students based on race and cultural similarities. Wallace and Bell (1999) revealed that students struggled to negotiate their feelings of racial discrimination at PWIs. The researchers explain that affirmative action programs in higher education provided greater access and opportunity for minority students to attend PWIs. However, according to Wallace and Bell (1999), as part of attending a PWI where racial marginalization is both explicit and implicit, students struggle to excel in an environment that was not intended for them in the first place.

In our study, the students explained their perceptions about the cultural climate differences between HBCUs and PWIs. In particular, when asked about social and cultural differences that could exist between the two institutions, Dorothy shares: "[HBCUs are] more fun … I think maybe music playing. I don't know, more upbeat, lively. A white school may be more uptight." This statement might suggest that to some prospective Black students, PWIs are not culturally accommodating to African Americans. As noted, this point is also raised in the literature that suggests that Black students express feelings of racial isolation, disconnectedness, and feelings of marginalization at PWIs (Schwitzer et al., 1999; Wallace & Bell, 1999).

Some of our participants (Troy, Kim, and Elisha) noted that they were able to understand what a Black college experience was by visiting HBCUs. However, it should be noted that there were few opportunities for college campus visits that were provided by high schools. Students were able to visit HBCUs through external organizations and or family members. Thus, high schools must do more to help students gain greater exposure to HBCUs. This is important. Some of the students in our study commented that they saw themselves as "fitting in" at an HBCU, having "more freedom," and being around people who were "actually intellectual." In this sense, HBCU campus visits helped the participants to see the value of these institutions and helped them feel a sense of cultural and racial belonging in a comfortable learning environment with educated Black people. It seems that with increased exposure to HBCUs, students are able to develop more concrete perceptions about these institutions.

However, some of our participants recognized that campus visits reinforced negative perceptions about HBCUs. For example, Elisha discusses his campus visit to Winston-Salem State University and explains that for him, the neighborhood was "raggedy." Elisha explains, "Well, the violence and stuff that's up there, because where Winston Salem is located is really a bad area where a lot of people get killed and stuff by the locals." Elisha's comments about the location of some HBCUs are actually based on the realities of U.S.' race relations, neighborhood segregation, urban sprawl, gentrification, and the disappearance of jobs in urban communities. These issues have deeply impacted African American neighborhoods and the institutions that serve these communities (Ainsworth, & Wiggan, 2006; Darling-Hammond, 2010; Du Bois, 1899; Kozol, 2005; Parker, 1998).

MEDIA IS IMPORTANT

The role of the media is also particularly important in this study because it has served as one of the primary influences on how students perceive HBCUs, and how they understand the Black college experience. The participants in the study mentioned two movies (*Drumline* and *Stomp the Yard*) in particular. For example, regarding *Drumline* and *Stomp the Yard*, the participants acknowledged that the movies showcased HBCUs in a positive light by demonstrating how relatable, personable, and family-oriented the colleges were. It is fitting to mention that studies indicate that strong Black identities can be forged through positive media depictions (Means-Coleman, 2002; Sun et al., 2002; Wood, 2002). However, it can also be argued that movies like *Drumline* and *Stomp the Yard* only illustrate the social side of HBCUs and they do not capture the historical and intellectual traditions of these institutions.

There are possible negative consequences of the media in showcasing the experiences of marching bands and fraternities, because these movies reinforce negative perceptions of HBCUs as party schools instead of institutions of academic excellence (Cantey et al., 2012). One participant (Elise) recognized a scene in *Stomp the Yard* that effectively captured the historical legacy of HBCUs with its acknowledgement of the leaders and important people who attended the institution. This minor scene in the movie stood out to Elise. For her, it demonstrated how HBCUs serve as a constant reminder of the legacy and inherited right that Black people have to education (Clarke, 1977). This clip was intentional, but perhaps not as impactful to moviegoers because it was only a brief instance where ancestors were paid homage.

Pertaining to African and African American heritage and ancestral contributions, Asante (2009) and Delpit and Dowdy (2002) note that the Eurocentric view of Blacks or the "othering" of African Americans in particular, by the dominant group has negative consequences in terms of how African Americans may view themselves or social institutions that are intended to serve them. The participants in our study have been exposed to this process. They commented on the differences between PWIs and HBCUs, but they generally felt that PWIs were more serious schools, and that they were better in quality.

In this light though, the students' interests in attending an HBCU was still sparked by the aforementioned movies *Stomp the Yard* and *Drumline*, in a way that at least exposed them to Black institutions. This may have been an unintended consequence of two popular films that were originally intended to showcase the social side and entertainment activities of Black colleges. Perhaps the directors and producers wanted to illustrate the cultural differences that exist between HBCUs and PWIs, but specifically in terms of Greek life and band life. Indeed, there is a difference that exists between "Black Greeks" and "White Greeks" and "show bands" and "concert bands." Until the production of these blockbusters, this was an area of college life that cinema or the main screen had not deeply explored from an African American perspective.

Kim, who mentioned BET, which is one of the primary outlets where African American teens receive their socialization about the world, discussed the program *106 & Park,* which occasionally showcases Black colleges. However, when the program is taped at a Black college or university (generally twice a year), it is always related to entertainment. More specifically, Hip Hop and R&B artists perform while disc jockeys (DJs) play music and entertain a crowd of college-goers. There are also celebrity hosts who facilitate random activities such as talent shows, trivia games, stepping, and strut or dance competitions.

In this sense, Black television programs such as *106 & Park* may be less relevant to the positive aspects of the exposure that African American teens receive about HBCUs. The 1990s television programming of *A Different World*, *The Cosby Show*, and Spike Lee films, which carried a social and educational theme relating to Black colleges, is long gone. Movies such as *School Daze* [1988] celebrated and critiqued Black colleges for their social and cultural traditions, *Do the Right Thing* [1989] and *House Party 2* [1991], which highlighted college life and the school-work balance, and *Higher Learning* [1995] which exposed race relations at PWIs, are not known to – or may even be an afterthought to the newest generation of Black students. Perhaps these movies are too dated for 21st century college-bound teens to reference and relate to. However, these movies were among the few that attempted to more fully capture the Black collegian experience. However, there are more recent movies, such as *The Great Debaters* [2007] and *From the Rough* [2014] that showcase students from HBCUs.

As a related issue, Elisha, a student in the study, discussed how HBCUs receive little sports coverage while in contrast, PWIs are highlighted in the media. He expresses that the games of Division I schools are aired on ESPN regularly. However, only major events and championship games of HBCUs are showcased on sister stations of the major network. The whole phenomenon of Black athletes playing for Division I institutions provide PWIs with greater media exposure and branding in positive ways, which promote more awareness and popularity among Black college-bound students, while concurrently diminishing the athletic programs and the branding that HBCUs would otherwise receive. Sponsorship of Black star athletes who play in Division I athletic programs also help contribute funding to PWIs that again, HBCUs would have otherwise received if these students were attending them.

RETURNS ON THE DEGREE

Our participants generally believed that HBCUs will provide them with greater cultural awareness than they would receive at a PWI. While many White and Black institutions still privilege Greek life (fraternities and sororities) and Eurocentric curricula and experiences, the students recognize that HBCUs are more likely to provide them with a culturally responsive education. This finding is supported by the existing literature that discusses how HBCUs are institutions that build cultural capital, provide a nurturing environment for the development of positive identities (Asante, 1998; Bourdieu, 1977; Cokley & Chapman, 2008; Davis, 1998; Rucker & Gendrin, 2003), and they create greater cultural awareness among students (Davis, 2004; Franklin & Savage, 2004).

Nevertheless, the issue of the return on the degree was a key consideration for the students in our study. The students' comments about what they perceived as limited employment opportunities they might receive with an HBCU degree can be viewed in terms of the fact that Whites generally have higher employment rates than their Black peers with the same degree and level of experience. For example, in 2012, the unemployment rate for African Americans with a bachelor's degree was 6%, compared to 3.5% for college-educated Whites (JBHE, 2015). Additionally, perhaps for our participants, they see many more Black college graduates of PWIs who hold high positions than HBCU graduates, and this might influence their perceptions on which school to attend. The students might have been unaware that people like television mogul Oprah Winfrey, Nobel Prize winners Toni Morrison and Alice Walker, Film Producer and Director Spike Lee, former Surgeon General David Satcher, Singer Erykah Badu, and Rapper Common, among others, are all HBCU graduates. While these are exceptions, people who attended Black schools and have also become famous, there must be a more concerted effort on the part of HBCUs to highlight the success of their graduates. This will help prospective students in their decision-making regarding what school to attend.

WHAT IS IMPORTANT TO PROSPECTIVE STUDENTS?

Since Black graduates of PWIs are more visible to college-bound students, and since many high schools do not share information about HBCUs with students, this may indirectly suggest to college-bound African American students that they will receive more returns on their college degree if they attend a PWI (Dillon, 1999; Tobolowsky et al., 2005). The perceived differences in the institutional returns on college degrees when buttressed with the backdrop of anti-Black race relations in the U.S., may explain why some of our interviewees said that race was not important to them in their school choice. Jimmy explains this issue when commenting on whether race was important in his decision making. He states: "No because I don't feel like me being black–as long as I'm getting an education, as long as I'm where

I want to be at, it shouldn't matter just because I'm Black." Shane adds to this sentiment: "Really, [race] doesn't affect me. I could see myself at any school, but it just has to be the right feeling." Furthermore, Kim mentions: "I feel like I can go to any college I want and excel." It should be reiterated that Jimmy, Shane, and Kim are not attending HBCUs after completing high school. Similarly, Judy discusses the issue of race in her decision on which college to attend:

> I don't think it impacted my decision, because, I mean, I don't really look at race so hard, like most of my friends are white, so, you know, plus, see I don't like being around black students here or anywhere else, but they're just like, sometimes more inappropriate, or do like, be mean to be upset or mad or something, I just find it pointless. And they just, they make fun of me anyways… It's really stupid.

Although the participants mention that HBCUs were "a good choice," race was not the key issue for them in deciding which college to attend. Additionally, each of the participants indicated no preference in which institutional type they were applying to. Therefore, they applied to both PWIs, HBCUs, and in the case of Jimmy, community college.

The students expressed conclusively that issues of race relations are still alive in the U.S. Yet, it was not their primary consideration in their college selection, but it was something that they were conscious of. What did matter most for the students was the cost of the school, its institutional reputation, the opportunity to obtain scholarships and funding, and employment outcomes by institutional type [HBCU vs. PWI]. Although many Black students are choosing PWIs based on their cost, popularity and reputation, many of the students in our study believed that they would actually do better or have better academic performance and greater support if they attended an HBCU rather than a PWI. This finding is consistent with the existing research on higher education performance and indicators of success among Black students (Albritton, 2012; Fountaine, 2012; Outcalt & Skewes-Cox, 2002; Thompson, 2008; Torres & Massey, 2012). Similarly, students recognized that they could possibly have different experiences depending on the support systems offered and utilized from the two institutions. This finding is similar to Schwitzer et al. (1999) who found that in PWIs, White faculty members had fewer interactions with their Black students. The lack of interactions between White faculty and Black students in PWIs is further complicated by the fact that Black students clearly recognize that White institutional branding had more currency than HBCUs did in the labor market. Cultural hegemony and White privilege in the workplace are ongoing phenomena that influence some students' decisions to attend PWIs. Therefore, HBCUs must play a greater role in preparing students to negotiate race relations and employment dynamics in the American social landscape. Although all of our participants valued the rich cultural traditions of HBCUs and the supportive environment, yet many of them were still willing to navigate the lack of support and the institutional racism they believed they might encounter in PWIs, with the hope of receiving a more affordable education from an institution with a strong reputation, and greater employment opportunities, which they perceived that a PWI could offer.

RECOMMENDATIONS

The findings of our study indicate that most Black students continue to have generally positive perceptions about HBCUs (Davis, 1998, 2004; Pitre, 2006). However, there is a greater need for state and federal governments to increase resources for HBCUs, both private and public (Fester et al., 2012; Gasman, 2006, 2007; Matthews & Hawkins, 2006). Additionally, each HBCU should develop a Grant and External Funding Office. The staff in this office should have the principal role of applying for external funding in the form of grants and donations. Most universities have a "grants office" and each month the staff applies for various grants, which often translates into millions of dollars in annual funding. In addition, the faculty should also be encouraged to apply for grants for their departments and programs. This would certainly help with the financial stability of HBCUs. Furthermore, independent Black institutions such as churches and other organizations should increase their contributions to HBCUs (Anderson, 1988), which historically, was one of the strengths of the Black church during the Reconstruction period (Wiggan, 2011). This is reminiscent of Anderson's (1988) treaties on the historical and now–contemporary role of independent Black churches in helping to support higher education for African Americans. However, in the 21st century, financial support to HBCUs through independent Black churches has been dwindling, and is not as strong as it was during the Reconstruction period and the first-half of the 20th century (Franklin & Savage, 2004; Wiggan, 2011). The lack of support for Black institutions of higher learning by the 21st century Black church has had a negative effect on the financial wellbeing and enrollment of HBCUs. In this sense, some of our participants perceived PWIs as having higher standards and as being leading institutions with strong reputations, whereas they saw HBCUs in terms of being underfunded, under supported, and being in poor neighborhoods (as mentioned by Kim, Jimmy, and Dorothy).

It is also important to note that the students in our study who participated in a Black college tour, did not do so through their high schools. Therefore, this suggests that college recruitment officers and high school counselors should do more to expose high school students to HBCUs and arrange more college tours and campus visits (Gyapong & Smith, 2012). Students who went on Black college tours were more likely to attend an HBCU. Therefore, it is recommended that each HBCU partner with at least 50 high schools to help supply the institution with a continuous pipeline of new students. These partnerships should seek to enhance students' college readiness and their exposure to college-level courses (Freeman, 1999; Freeman & Thomas, 2002). HBCUs should target Black high schools more strategically to ensure that they have ongoing student enrollments. Additionally, social media, popular press, and television programming are places where HBCUs can embed themselves to create greater positive visibility and exposure to potential students.

It is also recommended that Black alumni associations should play more active roles in HBCU recruitment initiatives and fundraising for these institutions. These graduates provide some of the best testimonials about HBCUs. Kim's grandmother and Moesha's father graduated from HBCUs. However, the majority of the students in our study would be first generation college-goers. In this sense, if these students become HBCU graduates, it would create deeper intergenerational transmissions of educational capital to future generations and the Black community in general. HBCUs and their alumni associations should also work together to create greater partnerships with businesses, corporations, non-profits, non-governmental organizations and other groups to help provide internships and employment opportunities for students. By building and strengthening these partnerships and connections, students will have more opportunities to explore different career fields, as well as gain employment. HBCUs must also be more deliberate in showcasing their graduates and increasing their presence in public spaces.

Our interviewees noted that one of the unique characteristics of HBCUs was that they offered greater exposure to African American history and culture. This exposure is not generally offered in the traditional high school curriculum, something which prospective students are seeking. Therefore, HBCUs must embrace this role and offer more Africana and Black studies curricula, as well as do more community engagement work. In some HBCUs, they do not have an Africana Studies Department, and this is rather disheartening and problematic when considering the struggles surrounding Black history and the rich intellectual traditions of Africans and African Americans. This is unacceptable and something that every HBCU must address. The curriculum and pedagogy in all departments and programs must connect to the historical and contemporary African Diaspora. Additionally, HBCUs must continue to increase their service to Black communities. In this way, these institutions can help to transform urban communities in America in the 21st century, as they did in the late 19th and early 20th centuries. In spite of the important role that HBCUs have played—and continue to play, because of integration, accreditation concerns, and declining financial resources, the future of HBCUs, *the last of the Black titans*, still remains uncertain in the 21st century.

Recommendations at a Glance

- State and federal governments should increase funding and resources for HBCUs [both private and public]
- Each HBCU should create a Grant and External Funding Office and aggressively apply for grants and other sources of external funding
- Faculty members should also be encouraged to apply for department and program grants [perhaps incentives could also be offered to faculty who apply for grants]
- Each HBCU should conduct independent accreditation reviews and compliance assessments
- Independent Black institutions such as churches should increase their contributions to HBCUs
- HBCUs should work together to increase the number of Black college tours and enhance the dissemination of institutional information to school counselors
- HBCUs should organize themselves and hold quarterly meetings to develop strategies to help ensure each other's success
- Each HBCU should partner with at least 50 high schools to help increase the pipeline of prospective students
- Black alumni associations should play a more active role in HBCUs [in recruitment, fund raising, and creating employment opportunities for students]
- HBCUs should create more business partnerships to help students gain meaningful work experiences

- HBCUs should increase the use of social media and television advertisements to attract prospective students
- HBCUs should showcase the success of their graduates in public spaces
- Each HBCU should develop a strong Africana Studies and Black Studies curricula – that connects to continental Africa and the Diaspora
- HBCUs should increase their service to Black communities – this is one sure way of maintaining a positive image and presence in communities and attract future students

In conclusion, the findings of our investigation reveal that college-bound African American teens' perceptions about attending an HBCU are generally positive. The students recognize how culturally enriching and academically supportive HBCUs are for African Americans (Albritton, 2012; Fountaine, 2012; Fries-Britt & Turner, 2002; Outcalt & Skewes-Cox, 2002; Thompson, 2008). However, these characteristics alone were not enough to shape their opinions about attending an HBCU. Students weighed heavily finances, institutional reputation, and their field of study in their consideration of which type of institution to attend. The students revealed that with regard to attending an HBCU, their decisions are further constrained by broader social, institutional and workforce dynamics, which privileges PWIs over HBCUs. Despite popular claims that the 21st century can be characterized as a post-racial society, the students' decision-making process reflects the continuing influence of White privilege.

Notwithstanding this, the students felt that they could potentially perform better in a majority-Black institution of higher learning, but funding was still a key issue for them. Therefore, when given the option of going to an HBCU or a PWI, beyond financial considerations and institutional reputation, the students appeared to have preferred an HBCU. Yet, these students were forced to think through their future prospects and which institutional degree would better enhance their life chances. Here again enters White privilege and the issue of being a minority in a majority White country. This too perhaps suggests that HBCUs are still important in helping students to understand and mediate against institutional racism and barriers and challenges they will face in society, as well as the workplace. Shane's comment, "I think HBCUs are a good choice, first choice, in my opinion," resonates that these institutions still play an important social role for African Americans in the 21st century.

This study contributes to the literature on African American students' perceptions about attending college and more specifically, an HBCU. Since the Freeman study (1999), there has been limited research on how Black students perceive higher education institutions and what factors influence them to attend. The current study provides insight on how family/peer influences, institutional characteristics and reputation, and media depictions of HBCUs serve to either encourage or deter Black student enrollment. However, there are questions that remain to be answered which provide rationale for future research. There is a need for longitudinal studies on Black students that span from their high school to the completion of their undergraduate degrees. These studies would provide more research on teens' perceptions in comparison to their actual experiences in a postsecondary institution.

Today, African Americans have many choices among colleges and universities they can attend. This is a testament to the progress that has been made in educational opportunity and access. However, while many HBCUs are closing and their missions are gradually changing, these schools continue to play a vital role in the education of African Americans.

APPENDICES

APPENDIX A: RECRUITMENT FLIER

Share your Perspectives on Choosing to Attend a

HISTORICALLY BLACK COLLEGE OR UNIVERSITY

Are YOU:

African American?
High School Student?
Currently enrolled in a public North Carolina school?

WE WANT YOU!!!!

As part of a research study that will be conducted as a dissertation project in affiliation with J. Willis University, we are recruiting African Americans enrolled in a North Carolina public high school to participate in two individual interviews that will allow them to share their beliefs and attitudes about attending a Historically Black College or University (HBCU).

If you are interested in participating, contact ________ at [redacted]

APPENDIX B: RECRUITMENT SCRIPT

As part of a research study that will be conducted at J. Willis University, we are recruiting African American students enrolled in a North Carolina public high school to participate in two individual semi-structured interviews that will allow them to share their beliefs and attitudes about attending a Historically Black College or University (HBCU). An HBCU is a college or university that caters to the African American student population, but welcomes people from all ethnic groups to enroll and attend.

HBCU institutions were, in pastime, the only means for African Americans to have access to and attain higher education degrees (Anderson, 1988). However, after the Reconstruction Period (1865–1877) and landmark legislation, there was a push for racial integration in schools and universities, and school choice and the availability of opportunities greatly influenced the number of African American students who chose to attend HBCUs. Today, there is total of 105 historically Black institutions across the nation since 1837 (Jackson, 2001; National Center for Education Statistics -NCES, 2009). Despite this fact, the U.S. Department of Education only recognizes ninety-nine institutions, however, due to national accreditation standards set. NCES (2012) reported that there are over 330,000 students enrolled in HBCUs; however, only 78 percent account for the African American student population; which is a decline in overall Black student enrollment since earlier decades with the Black student population accounting for nearly 90 percent of the schools (NCES, 2009). Added, the total number of African Americans enrolled in U.S. accredited institutions is approximately 3 million, but only 9 percent of those students are enrolled in HBCUs.

Additionally, with financial issues, accreditation concerns, negative media attention, and overall lower enrollment ratings, much attention has put today's HBCUs in jeopardy. From the historical context of education for African American students that is premised in HBCUs, there is a need to examine contemporary perspectives on their significance. This study seeks to examine the perspectives of college-bound African American teens on attending an HBCU. With dwindling enrollment ratings for HBCUs, this study seeks to investigate if HBCUs serve as a mecca for cultural capital through the perspectives of college-bound African American students. It is important to understand important factors that may contribute to the shaping perspectives of Black teens on attending HBCUs: (1) racial identity and development; (2) an HBCU's cultural capital; and (3) current issues facing HBCUs.

Students that agree to participate will be asked to take part in two-individual in-person interviews outside of school that could last up to 2 hours. These interviews will take place January 2013 through December 2013 and will be scheduled at the convenience (time, date, and location) of the student and their parents. This study has nothing to do with your school and teachers at the school. Students will not receive a grade for participating in the study. The study will not affect your grades in school. The interview will be audio recorded so that I confirm I have an accurate account of what was said during the interview. I will store these recordings in my locked office in a locked cabinet until the study is complete. After the study is complete, I will destroy all the recordings by deleting them.

If you choose to volunteer to participate, you will be provided with the see parental consent, student assent and student consent forms (your teacher, administrator, or school front office will have them available). If you are under 18 years of age, a parent/guardian will need to consent to your participation. If you are 18 years of age or older, you will need to simply complete the student consent form. We will then contact you at a later date and set up an interviewing time that will be most convenient for you.

Your participation in this study will not affect your participation with school in any way. The decision to participate in this study is completely up to you. There are questions that will be asked about your race/ethnicity and cultural background. If you decide to be in the study, you may stop at any time or you can choose not to answer particular questions if you feel uncomfortable doing so. You will not be treated any differently if you decide not to participate in the study or if you stop once you have started.

All of the documents and data collected in the interviews will not contain information that can identify you. The findings for the study will be used for a dissertation project and will also be used subsequently to further inform the field of educational research surrounding Black student perceptions on choosing to attend an HBCU. If you decide to be in the study, you may stop at any time. You will not be treated any differently if you decide not to participate in the study or if you stop once you have started. Your name will not be used in any part of the study to protect your identity.

APPENDIX C: STUDENT INFORMATION SHEET

Name: ____________________ Pseudonym Assigned: _______________
Grade Level: ______________ Phone Number: ____________________
Age: ______________________ Email Address: ____________________
Name of High School Attending: ______________________________
Extra-Curricular Activities (if any): ___________________________
Do you plan to attend a college or university? (Please circle one.)YES NO
If you answered yes, please list colleges/universities you are considering and why:

____
____
____
____

What is your "dream college" to attend? ___________________________
What is your anticipated major in college? _________________________
What do you hope to become after graduating from college? ___________
Have you received any type of college preparation or readiness? YES NO
If you answered yes, please list who/what helped you to prepare for college:

____
____

Are there any members of your family who have attended or currently attend college? If so, please list them, the college in which they attend/attended, and their profession.

____
____

Is there anyone in particular who has inspired you to attend college? ______
Is there anyone who has attended college that has inspired you? __________

APPENDIX D: INTERVIEW PROTOCOL

INTERVIEW 1

Section I: The Importance of the 'Black College Experience'

1. Do you know what a Historically Black College and University (HBCU) is?
2. How is an HBCU different from a Predominately White Institution (PWI)?
3. Do you know anyone who has attended an HBCU? If so, did you talk to them about their experience?
4. Have you ever visited an HBCU?
5. Did anyone from your family attend an HBCU?
6. How does your race impact your decisions in attending college?
7. What does it mean to have the 'Black College Experience?'
8. In your opinion, how important is it to go to an HBCU?
9. Do you think attending an HBCU would help you to learn more about African American culture? Why or why not?
10. Do you think you would academically perform better at an HBCU? Why or why not?

Section II: The Perception and Attitude about attending an HBCU

1. What's your general opinion about attending an HBCU?
2. Have you seen anything on TV that tells you about HBCUs?
3. Do you know of any cultural differences that could exist at an HBCU and a PWI?
4. Do you know of any academic differences that could exist at an HBCU and a PWI?
5. Do you know of any social differences that could exist at an HBCU and a PWI?
6. Can you give me any reasons why you think attending an HBCU would be an advantage?
7. Can you give me any reasons why you think attending an HBCU would be a disadvantage?

INTERVIEW 2

1. Have you learned or heard of anything else about HBCUs since we last spoke?
2. Have you visited any HBCUs since we last spoke?
3. Do you know of any famous people who have graduated or attended HBCUs?
4. What's your general opinion about attending an HBCU?
5. Do you know of any differences that could exist at an HBCU and a PWI?
6. What influences your decision about attending an HBCU?

BIBLIOGRAPHY

African American Registry. (2000). *Richard Allen, Bishop, AME's first leader*. Retrieved from http://www.aaregistry.org/historic_events/view/richard-allen-bishop-ames-first-leader

African Kingdoms. (n.d.). *Kingdoms of Africa: Cradle of civilizations and humanity*. Retrieved from http://www.africankingdoms.com/

Africanus, L., Al-Wezaz Al-Faski, A., Porky, J., & Brown, R. (1600). *The history and description of Africa and of the notable things therein contained*. London, England: Hakluyt Society.

Ainsworth, J., & Wiggan, G. (2006). Why neighborhoods matter: How neighborhood context can shape educational and individual outcomes across racial groups. In E. McNamara Horvat & C. O'Connor, (Eds.), *Beyond acting White: Reassessments and new directions in research on Black students and school success* (pp. 159–175). New York, NY: Rowan & Littlefield.

Albritton, T. J. (2012). Educating our own: The historical legacy of HBCUs and their relevance for educating a new generation of scholars. *Urban Review*, *44*, 311–331. doi:10.1007/s11256-012-0202-9

Alkalimat, A., Bailey, R., Byndom, S., McMillon, D., Nesbitt, L., Williams, K., & Zelip, B. (2013). *African American studies 2013: A national web-based survey*. Urbana, IL: University of Illinois at Urbana Champaign Department of African American Studies. Retrieved from http://afro.illinois.edu

American Baptist Home Mission Societies. (2007). *Where we come from*. Retrieved from http://www.abhms.org/come_from.cfm

Amherst College. (n.d.). *A history of Amherst college*. Retrieved from http://www1.amherst.edu/about_amh06/history/index.html

Anderson, J. D. (1988). *The education of Blacks in the south, 1860–1935*. Chapel Hill, NC: The University of North Carolina Press.

Anderson, E., & Moss, A. A. (1999). *Dangerous donations: Northern philanthropy and southern Black education, 1902–1930*. Columbia, MO: University of Missouri Press.

Asante, M. K. (1998). *The Afrocentric idea*. Philadelphia, PA: Temple University Press.

Asante, M. K. (2009). *Afrocentricity*. Retrieved from http://www.asante.net/articles/1/afrocentricity/

AU Collection. (1800s). Beginnings of education among the freedmen in Atlanta. *Atlanta University Collection* 87-007-03.001. Atlanta, GA: Robert W. Woodruff Library Archives.

Awokoya, J., Richards, D., & Myrick-Harris, C. (2012). *Serving students and the public good: HBCUs and the Washington monthly's college rankings*. Fairfax, VA: Frederick D. Patterson Research Institute, UNCF.

Bell, D. A. (1989). The final report: Harvard's affirmative action allegory. *Michigan Law Review*, *87*, 2382–2410.

Bell, D. A. (1992). *Faces at the bottom of the well: The permanence of racism*. New York, NY: Basic Books.

Bio. (2015). *Famous Harlem renaissance people*. Retrieved from http://www.biography.com/people/groups/movement-harlem-renaissance

Bourdieu, P. (1977). Cultural reproduction and social reproduction. In K. Karabel & A. H. Halsey (Eds.), *Power and ideology in education* (pp. 487–511). New York, NY: Oxford University Press.

Bowdoin College Library. (n.d.). *Africana studies resources.* Retrieved from http://library.bowdoin.edu/arch/subject-guides/africana-resources/john-brown-russwurm/index.shtml

Braddock II, J. M., & Hua, L. (2006). Determining the college destination of African American high school seniors: Does college athletic reputation matter? *Journal of Negro Education, 75*, 532–545.

Brown, M. M. (1989). What are the qualities of good research? In F. H. Hultgren & D. L. Coomer (Eds.), *Alternate modes of inquiry in home economics research: Yearbook 9, American home economics association* (pp. 257–297). Peoria, IL: Glencoe Publishing Company.

Brown, M. C., Ricard, R., & Donahoo, S. (2004). The changing role of historically Black colleges and universities: Vistas on dual missions, desegregation, and diversity. In M. C. Brown & K. Freeman (Eds.), *Black colleges: New perspectives on policy and practice* (pp. 3–28). Westport, CT: Praeger.

Campus Connections, B. C. T. Inc. (n.d.). *About us.* Retrieved from http://www.campusconnections.org/aboutus.html

Cantey, N. I., Bland, R., Mack, L. R., & Joy-Davis, D. (2012). Historically Black colleges and universities: Sustaining a culture of excellence in the twenty-first century. *Journal of African American Studies, 17*, 142–153. doi:10.1007/s12111-011-9191-0

Carwardine, R. (2000, September). Methodists, politics, and the coming of the American civil war. *Church History, 69*(3), 578–609.

Chambers, J. (2015). *NC HBCUs struggle with finances, enrollment.* Retrieved from http://www.wral.com/-fightingtosurvive-nc-hbcus-struggle-with-financesenrollment/14372354/

Chavous, T., Rivas, D., Green, L., & Helaire, L. (2002). Role of student background, perceptions of ethnic fit, and racial identification in the academic adjustment of African American students at a predominately White university. *Journal of Black Psychology, 28*(3), 234–260. doi:10.1177/0095798402028003004

Cheyney University. (2015). *History of Cheyney university.* Retrieved from http://www.cheyney.edu/about-cheyney-university/cheyney-history.cfm

Clarke, J. H., Jackson, E., Kaiser, E., & O'Dell, J. H. (1970). *Black titan W. E. B. Du Bois: An anthology by the editors of freedom ways.* Boston, MA: Beacon Press.

Clarke, J. H. (June, 1977). The university of Sankore at Timbuctoo: A neglected achievement in Black intellectual history. *The Western Journal of Black Studies, 1*(2), 142–146.

Clarke, J. (1993). *Christopher Columbus and the Afrikan Holocaust: Slavery and the rise of European capitalism.* New York, NY: A&B Publishers Group.

Cokley, K.O., & Chapman, C. (2008). The roles of ethnic identity, anti-White attitudes, and academic self-concept in African American student achievement. *Social Psychology of Education, 11*, 349–365. doi:10.007/s11218-008-9060-4

Dancy, T. E., & Brown, C. (2008). Unintended consequences: African American male educational attainment and collegiate perceptions after brown v. board of education. *American Behavioral Scientist, 51*(7), 984–1003. doi:10.1177/0002764207312001

Darling-Hammond, L. (2010). *The flat world and education: How America's commitment to equity will determine our future.* New York, NY: Teachers College Press.

Davidson, B. (1964). *The African past: Chronicles from antiquity to modern times.* Boston, MA: Little, Brown.

Davis, J. E. (1998). Cultural capital and the role of historically Black colleges and universities in educational reproduction. In K. Freeman (Ed.), *African American cultural and heritage in higher education research and practice* (pp. 143–153). Westport, CT: Praeger.

Davis, R. D. (2004). *Black students' perceptions: The complexity of persistence to graduation at an American university*. New York, NY: Peter Lang.

Davis Jr. L. A. (2006). Success against the odds: The HBCU experience. In F. W. Hale, Jr. (Ed.), *How Black colleges empower Black students: Lessons for higher education* (pp. 43–50). Sterling, VA: Stylus.

DECA. (n.d.). *About us*. Retrieved from http://www.deca.org/about/

Delgado, R. (1990). When a story is just a story: Does voice really matter? *Virginia Law Review*, *76*, 95–111.

Delpit, L. D. (1988). The silenced dialogue: Power and pedagogy in educating other people's children. *Harvard Educational Review*, *58*(3), 280–299.

Delpit, L. D. (1995). *Other people's children: Cultural conflict in the classroom*. New York, NY: The New Press.

Delpit, L. D., & Dowdy, J. K. (Eds.). (2002).*The skin that we speak: Thoughts on language and culture in the classroom*. New York, NY: The New Press.

Dillon, D. W. (1999). *Perceptions of Louisiana high school students toward selected university types: Predominately White institutions and historically Black institutions of higher education* (Doctoral dissertation). Baton Rouge, LA: Louisiana State University.

Diop, C. A. (1974). *The African origin of civilization: Myth or reality*. New York, NY: L. Hill.

Distinguished Young Gentlemen of America (DYG). (n.d.). *National summer academy*. Retrieved from http://www.dygofamerica.org/nsa

Douglas, K. B. (1998). Impressions: African American first-year students' perceptions of a predominately White university. *The Journal of Negro Education*, *67*(4), 416–431.

Du Bois, W. E. B. (1899/1996). *The Philadelphia Negro: A social study*. Philadelphia, PA: University of Pennsylvania Press.

Du Bois, W. E. B. (1903). *The souls of Black folk*. Chicago, IL: A.C. McClurg & Co.

Du Bois, W. E. B. (1935). *Black reconstruction: An essay toward a history of the part which Black folk played in the attempt to reconstruct democracy in America, 1860–1880*. New York, NY: Harcourt, Brace & Company.

Du Bois, W. E. B., & Dill, A. G. (Eds.). (1910). *The college-bred Negro American*. Atlanta, GA: Atlanta University Press.

Eder, D., & Fingerson, L. (2003). Interviewing children and adolescents. In J. A. Holstein & J. F. Gubrium (Eds.), *Inside interviewing: New lenses, new concerns* (pp. 33–53). Thousand Oaks, CA: Sage.

Encyclopedia Britannica. (2014). *Reconstruction*. Retrieved from http://www.britannica.com/EBchecked/topic/493722/Reconstruction

Erickson, F. (1992). Why the clinical trial doesn't work as a metaphor for educational research: A response to Schrag. *Educational Researcher*, *21*(5), 9–11.

Fenning, P., & Rose, J. (2007). Overrepresentation of African American students in exclusionary discipline: The role of school policy. *Urban Education*, *42*(6), 536–559.

Fester, R., Gasman, M., & Nguyen, T. (2012). We know very little: Accreditation and historically Black colleges and universities. *Journal of Black Studies*, *43*(7), 806–819. doi:10.1177/0021934712453467

Fields, M. M., & Murty, K. S. (2012). Private vs. public: The politics of access with opportunity. In V. R. Newkirk (Ed.), *New life for historically Black colleges and universities: A 21st century perspective* (pp. 70–96). Jefferson, NC: McFarland.

Fleming, J. (1984). *Blacks in college: A comparative study of students' success in Black and White institutions*. San Francisco, CA: Jossey-Bass.

Florida A., & M University. (n.d.). *Gallery of distinction inductees*. Retrieved from http://www.famu.edu/index.cfm?EssentialTheatre&GalleryofDistinction

Fountaine, T. P. (2012). The impact of faculty-student interaction on Black doctoral students attending historically Black institutions. *The Journal of Negro Education, 81*(2), 136–147

Franklin, V. P., & Savage, C. J. (Eds.). (2004). *Cultural capital and Black education: African American communities and the funding of Black schooling, 1865 to the present*. Greenwich, CT: Information Age Publishing.

Freeman, K. (1999). HBCUs or PWIs? African American high school students' consideration of higher education institution types. *Review of Higher Education, 23*(1), 91–106.

Freeman, K. (2005). *African Americans and college choice: The influence of family and school*. New York, NY: State University of New York Press.

Freeman, K., & Thomas, G. E. (2002). Black colleges and college choice: Characteristics of students who choose HBCUs. *Review of Higher Education, 25*(3), 349–358. doi:10.1353/rhe.2002.0011

Fries-Britt, S., & Turner, B. (2002). Uneven stories: Successful Black collegians at a Black and a White campus. *Review of Higher Education, 25*, 315–330.

Gasman, M. (2006). Salvaging "academic disaster areas": The Black college response to Christopher Jencks and David Riesman's 1967 Harvard educational review article. *The Journal of Higher Education, 77*(2), 317–352.

Gasman, M. (2007). Truths, generalizations, and stigmas: An analysis of the media's coverage of Morris Brown college and Black colleges overall. *Review of the Black Political Economy, 47*(1–2), 111–147. doi:10.1007/s12114-007-9001-z

Gasman, M., & Bowman, III. (2011). How to paint a better portrait of HBCUs. *Academe*. Retrieved from http://www.aaup.org/article/how-paint-better-portrait-hbcus#.UuSiAaMo6os

Girl Voice Network. (n.d.). *About our organization*. Retrieved from https://sites.google.com/site/girlvoicenetwork/about-our-organization

Giroux, H. A. (1994). Doing cultural studies: Youth and the challenge of pedagogy. *Harvard Education Review, 64*(3), 278–308. Retrieved from http://www.edreview.org/harvard94/1994/fa94/f94girou.htm

Gray, C. C. (2001). *Afrocentric thought and praxis: An intellectual history*. Trenton, NJ: African World Press.

Gyapong, S. K., & Smith, T. (2012). Factors influencing generation Y African Americans in their choice for college education: An empirical case study of fort valley state university students. *Contemporary Issues in Education, 5*(1), 39–46.

Habitat for Humanity. (n.d.). *Campus chapter four functions*. Retrieved 2014 from http://www.habitat.org/youthprograms/campus-chapters/four-functions

Harvard University Press. (n.d.). *The W. E. B. Du Bois lectures*. Retrieved from http://www.hup.harvard.edu/collection.php?cpk=1011

Herodotus. (2014). *The history of Herodotus* (Vol. 1, G. C. MacCaulay, Trans.). Lexington, KY: CreateSpace Independent Publishing Platform. (Original work published in 440 B.C.E.)

Hilliard, A. G. (1995). *The maroon within us: Selected essays on African American community socialization*. Baltimore, MD: Black Classic Press.

"History of Juneteenth". (n.d.). *In Juneteenth.com*. Retrieved from http://www.juneteenth.com/history.htm

Holmes, D. O. W. (1934). *The evolution of the Negro college*. College Park, MD: McGrath.

Howard University. (2013). *A letter of critique from a Howard university trustee*. Retrieved from http://www.washingtonpost.com/local/education/a-letter-of critique-from-a-howard-utrustee/2013/06/10/f3e81b9c-d1d3-11e2-a73e826d299ff459_story.html

HyperRESEARCH (Version 2.8) [Computer software]. Randolph, MA: ResearchWare.

Jackson, C. L. (2001). *African American education: A reference handbook*. Santa Barbara, CA: ABC-CLIO.

Journal of Blacks in higher education. (JBHE). (2015). *Unemployment rates of African Americans by bachelor's degree field*. Retrieved from http://www.jbhe.com/2015/03/unemployment-rates-of-africanamericans-by bachelors-degree-field/

Jencks, C., & Riesman, D. (1967). The American Negro college. *Harvard Educational Review*, *37*(2), 3–60.

Jhally, S., & Lewis, J. (1992). *Enlightened racism: The Cosby show, audiences, and the myth of the American dream*. Boulder, CO: Westview Press.

Johnson, D. Y. (2010). *African American/Black undergraduate students: Perceptions of their experiences attending an upper Midwest university* (Doctoral dissertation). University of North Dakota, Grand Forks, ND

Journal of Blacks in Higher Education (JBHE). (2013). *Key events in Black higher education: JBHE chronology of major landmarks in the progress of African Americans in higher education*. Retrieved from http://www.jbhe.com/chronology/

Journal of Blacks in Higher Education (JBHE). (2013). *News and views*. Retrieved from http://www.jbhe.com/news_views/64_degrees.html

Kim, M. M., & Conrad, C. F. (2006). The impact of historically Black colleges and universities on the academic success of African-American students. *Research in Higher Education*, *47*(4), 399–427. doi:10.1007/s11162-005-9001-4

Kim, J., DesJardins, S. L., & McCall, B. P. (2009). Exploring the effects of student expectations about financial aid on postsecondary choice: A focus on income and racial/ethnic differences. *Research in Higher Education*, *50*, 741–774. doi:10.1007/s11162-009-9143-x

Kozol, J. (2005). *The shame of a nation: The restoration of apartheid schooling in America*. New York, NY: Crown.

Kvale, S. (1996). *InterViews: An introduction to qualitative research interviewing*. Thousand Oaks, CA: Sage.

Ladson-Billings, G. (1994). *The dream-keepers: Successful teachers of African American children*. San Francisco, CA: Jossey-Bass.

Ladson-Billings, G. (1998). Just what is critical race theory and what's it doing in a nice field like education? *International Journal of Qualitative Studies in Education*, *11*(1), 7–24.

The Leadership Conference. (2014). *Brown vs. board of education*. The leadership conference on civil and human rights. Retrieved from http://www.civilrights.org/education/brown/

Lewin, T. (2012, March). Black students face more discipline, data suggests. *The New York Times*. Retrieved from http://www.nytimes.com/2012/03/06/education/Black-students-face-more-harsh-discipline-data-shows.html?_r=1

Library of Congress. (n.d.). Morrill act. *The Library of Congress*. Retrieved from http://www.loc.gov/rr/program/bib/ourdocs/Morrill.html
Lincoln University. (n.d.). *Langston Hughes class of 29*. Retrieved from http://www.lincoln.edu/library/abouthughes.html
Lincoln, Y. S., & Denzin, N. K. (2005). Introduction: The discipline and practice of qualitative research. In N. K. Denzin & Y. S. Lincoln (Eds.), *Handbook of qualitative research* (3rd ed., pp. 1–32). Thousand Oaks, CA: Sage.
Lincoln, Y. S., & Guba, E. G. (1985). *Naturalistic inquiry*. Beverly Hills, CA: Sage.
Lipman, P. (2004). *High stakes education: Inequality, globalization, and urban school reform*. New York, NY: Routledge.
Lovett, B. L. (2011). *America's historically Black colleges and universities: A narrative history: 1837–2009*. Macon, GA: Mercer University Press.
Madison High School. (n.d.). *Madison high school extracurricular activities: Clubs*. Retrieved from https://sites.google.com/a/mgsd.k12.nc.us/mhs-website-v1/extracurriculars/clubs
Martin Jr., W. E. (Ed.). (1998). *Brown v. board of education: A brief history with documents*. Boston, MA: Bedford/St. Martin's.
Matthews, F. L., & Hawkins, B. D. (2006). Black colleges: Still making an indelible impact with less. In F. W. Hale, Jr. (Ed.), *How Black colleges empower Black students: Lessons for higher education* (pp. 35–42). Sterling, VA: Stylus.
McGloster, N. (2015, February 11). The empire Taraji P. Henson built. *Uptown Magazine*. Retrieved from http://uptownmagazine.com/2015/02/empiretaraji-phenson-interview/
McLeod, H. (2015). *South Carolina state university close to being taken over by the state*. Retrieved from http://www.huffingtonpost.com/2015/02/19/sc-lawmakers advancepl_n_6716124.html
Means-Coleman, R. R. (Ed.). (2002). *Say it loud! African American audiences, media, and identity*. New York, NY: Routledge.
Merriam, S. B. (1998). *Qualitative research and case study applications in education*. San Francisco, CA: Jossey-Bass.
Minor, J. T. (2008). A contemporary perspective on the role of public HBCUs: Perspicacity from Mississippi. *Journal of Negro Education, 77*(4), 323–335.
Morehouse College. (n.d.). *King at Morehouse*. Retrieved from http://www.morehouse.edu/kingcollection/life.php
Morgan, H. (1995). *Historical perspectives on the education of Black children*. Westport, CT: Praeger.
Morrill, J. (2013, November 4). Watt, JCSU president rip federal loan policy. *The Charlotte Observer*. Retrieved from http://www.charlotteobserver.com/2013/11/04/4439592/watt-jcsu-president-rip-federal.html#.UtMGP7Eo7ct
Mullins, D. (2013). Historically Black colleges in financial fight for their future. Retrieved from http://america.aljazeera.com/articles/2013/10/22/historicallyBlackcollegesfightfortheirfuture.html
National Association for Equal Opportunity in Higher Education (NAFEO). (n.d.). *Welcome to NAFEO*. Retrieved from http://www.nafeo.org/community/index.php
National Association for the Advancement of Colored People (NAACP). (n.d.). *NAACP history: Charles Hamilton Houston*. Retrieved from http://www.naacp.org/pages/naacp-history-charles-hamilton-houston

Obenga, T. (1992). *Ancient Egypt & Black Africa: A student's handbook for the study of ancient Egypt in philosophy, linguistics, & gender relations*. Britain, England: Karnak House.

Office of Civil Rights. (1991). *Historically Black colleges and universities and higher education desegregation.* Office of civil rights, US and Department of education. Washington, DC. Retrieved from http://www2.ed.gov/about/offices/list/ocr/docs/hq9511.html

Outcalt, C. L., & Skewes-Cox, T. E. (2002). Involvement, interaction, and satisfaction: The human environment at HBCUs. *The Review of Higher Education, 25*(3), 331–347. doi:10.1353/rhe.2002.0015

Paddock, A. (2013). *Historically Black colleges are seeing an increase of White students.* Retrieved from http://www.washingtonpost.com/blogs/therootdc/post/historically Black-colleges are-seeing-an-increase-of-White-students/2013/05/17/5a642f5e bd80-11e2-89c93be8095fe767_blog.html

Parker, L. (1998). "Race is race ain't": An explanation of the utility of critical race theory in qualitative research in education. *International Journal of Qualitative Studies in Education, 11*(1), 42–55.

Parks, C. (2003, August). *Are HBCUs still necessary?* Retrieved from http://sciencecareers.sciencemag.org/career_magazine/previous_issues/articles/2003_08_22/nodoi.15268406798050218882

PBS [Public Broadcasting Service]. (2004). *No escape from slavery.* Retrieved from http://www.pbs.org/wnet/slavery/timeline/1662.html

Perna, L. W. (2000). Differences in the decision to attend college among African Americans, Hispanics, and Whites. *Journal of Higher Education, 71*, 117–141.

Perna, L. W. (2001). The contribution of historically Black colleges and universities to the preparation of African Americans for faculty careers. *Research in Higher Education, 42*, 267–294.

Perna, L., Lundy-Wagner, V., Drezner, N. D., Gasman, M., Yoon, S., Bose, E., & Gary, S. (2009). The contribution of HBCUs to the preparation of African American women for STEM careers: A case study. *Research in Higher Education, 50*, 1–23. doi:10.1007/s11162-008-9110-y

Perna, L. W., Milem, J., Gerald, D., Baum, E., Rowan, H., & Hutchens, N. (2006). The status of equity for Black undergraduates in public higher education in the south: Still separate and unequal. *Research in Higher Education, 47*(2), 197–228. doi:10.1007/s11162-005-8886-2

Peshkin, A. (1993). The goodness of qualitative research. *Educational Researcher, 22*(2), 23–29.

Phillips, D. C., & Burbules, N. C. (2000). *Postpositivism and educational research.* Lanham, MD: Rowman& Littlefield.

Pitre, P. E. (2006). College choice: A study of African American and White student aspirations and perceptions related to college attendance. *College Student Journal, 40*, 562–574.

Plutarch. (2012). *Parallel lives* (Vol. 1). Radford, VA: SMK Books. (Original work published in 75 C.E.)

Price, G. N., Spriggs, W., & Swinton, O. H. (2011). The relative returns to graduating from a historically Black college/university: Propensity score matching estimates from the national survey of Black Americans. *Review of the Black Political Economy, 38*, 103–130. doi:10.1007/s12114-011-9088-00

Redd, K. E. (2000). *HBCU graduates: Employment, earnings and success after college.* Indianapolis, IN: USA Group Foundation.

Richards, D. A. R., & Awokoya, J. T. (2012). *Understanding HBCU retention and completion.* Fairfax, VA: Frederick D. Patterson Research Institute, UNCF.

Rist, R. C. (1970). Student social class and teacher expectations: The self-fulfilling prophecy in ghetto education. *Harvard Educational Review, 40*(3), 411–451.

Rist, R. C. (2000). HER classic: Student social class and teacher expectations: The self fulfilling prophecy in ghetto education. *Harvard Educational Review, 70*(3), 257–265.

Ronald McDonald House of Charlotte. (n.d.). *Teen volunteer board and teen service corps.* Retrieved from http://www.rmhofcharlotte.org/how-you-can-help/volunteer/teen-volunteer-board

Rossman, G. B., & Rallis, S. F. (2003). *Learning in the field: An introduction to qualitative research.* Thousand Oaks, CA: Sage.

Rucker, M. L., & Gendrin, D. M. (2003). The impact of ethnic identification on student learning in the HBCU classroom. *Journal of Instructional Psychology, 30*(3), 207–215.

Saad, E. (1983). *Social history of Timbuktu: The role of Muslim scholars and notables 1400–1900.* New York, NY: Cambridge University Press.

Scardigli, B. (1995). *Essays on plutarch's lives.* Oxford, England: Clarendon Press.

Schwandt, T. A. (2007). *The Sage dictionary of qualitative inquiry* (3rd ed.). Los Angeles, CA: Sage.

Schwitzer, A. M., Griffin, O. T., Ancis, J. R., & Thomas, C. R. (1999). Social adjustment experiences of African American college students. *Journal of Counseling & Development, 77*, 189–197.

Smith, J. K. (1983). Quantitative versus qualitative research: An attempt to clarify the issue. *Educational Researcher, 12*(3), 6–13.

Snyder, T. D., & Dillow, S. A. (2012). *Digest of education statistics 2011* (NCES 2012–001). National center for education statistics, institute of education sciences, U.S. Department of Education. Washington, DC. Retrieved from http://nces.ed.gov/pubs2012/2012001_0.pdf

Solorzano, D. G. (1995). The doctorate production and baccalaureate origins of African Americans in the sciences and engineering. *Journal of Negro Education, 64*(1), 15–32.

Stuart, R. (2012, October 2). HBCUs facing challenges amid efforts to stay financially viable and competitive. *Diverse Issues in Higher Education.* Retrieved from http://diverseeducation.com/article/48471/

Students Preventing and Informing on Drugs and Alcohol (SPIDA). (n.d.). *Our mission.* Retrieved from http://www.spidacharlotte.org/

Sun, C. F., Cooks, L., Rinehart, C., & Williams, A. S. (2002). DMX, cosby, and two sides of the American dream. In R. R. Means-Coleman (Ed.), *Say it loud! African-American audiences, media, and identity* (pp. 115–145). New York, NY: Routledge.

Tate IV, W. F. (1997). Critical race theory and education: History, theory, and implications. *Review of Research in Education, 22*, 195–247. doi:10.3102/0091732X02201195

Thomas, B. (Ed.). (1997). *Plessy vs. Ferguson: A brief history with documents.* Boston, MA: Bedford/St. Martin's.

Thompson, P. F. (2008). On firm foundations: African American Black college graduates and their doctoral student development in the Ivy league. In M. Gasman & C. L. Tudico (Eds.), *Historically Black colleges and universities: Triumphs, troubles, and taboos* (pp. 27–40). New York, NY: Palgrave MacMillan.

Thurgood Marshall College Fund. (2012). *Justice Thurgood Marshall history.* Retrieved from https://www.thurgoodmarshallfund.net/about-tmcf/thurgood-marshallhistory

Thurgood Marshall Fund. (2015). About historically Black colleges and universities. Retrieved from https://www.thurgoodmarshallfund.net/about-tmcf/about-hbcus

Tobolowsky, B. F., Outcalt, C. L., & McDonough, P. M. (2005). The role of HBCUs in the college choice process of African Americans in California. *Journal of Negro Education, 74*(1), 63–75.

Torres, K., & Massey, D. S. (2012). Fitting in: Segregation, social class, and the experiences of Black students at selective colleges and universities. *Race and Social Problems, 4*(3–4), 171–192.

Traore, R., & Lukens, R. J. (2006). *This isn't the America I thought I'd find: African students in the urban U.S. high school.* Lanham, MD: University Press of America.

United Negro College Fund (UNCF). (2014). *About HBCUs.* Retrieved from http://www.uncf.org/sections/MemberColleges/SS_AboutHBCUs/about.hbcu.asp

United Negro College Fund (UNCF). (n.d.). *Who we are.* Retrieved from http://www.uncf.org/sections/WhoWeAre/index.asp

Upton, R., & Tanenbaum, C. (2014, September). *The role of historically Black colleges and universities as pathway providers: Institutional pathways to the STEM PhD among Black students.* Retrieved from http://www.air.org/sites/default/files/downloads/report/Role%20of%20HBCUs% 0in%0STEM%20PhDs%20for%20Black%20Students.pdf

U.S. Army Junior Reserve Officers' Training Corps (U.S. Army JROTC). (n.d.). *An overview of the JROTC.* Retrieved from http://www.usarmyjrotc.com/overview-of-jrotc

U.S. Commission on Civil Rights (2010). *The educational effectiveness of historically Black colleges and universities.* U.S. Commission on Civil Rights. Washington, DC. Retrieved from http://www.usccr.gov/pubs/HBCU_webversion2.pdf

U.S. Department of Education, National Center for Education Statistics (NCES). (1995). *Minority undergraduate participation in postsecondary education (NCES 95–166).* U.S. Department of education, Office of educational research and improvement. Washington, DC. Retrieved from http://nces.ed.gov/pubs95/95166.pdf

U.S. Department of Education, National Center for Education Statistics (NCES). (2004). *The condition of education, 2004 (NCES 2004–077).* Washington, DC: U.S. Government Printing Office.

U.S. Department of Education, National Center for Education Statistics (NCES). (2012). *Digest of education statistics, 2011 (NCES 2012–001).* Washington, DC: National Center for Education Statistics.

U.S. Department of Education, National Center for Education Statistics (NCES). (2013). *Digest of education statistics, 2012 (NCES 2014–015).* Washington, DC: National Center for Education Statistics.

van Camp, D., Barden, J., & Sloan, L. R. (2010). Predictors of Black students' race-related reasons for choosing an HBCU and intentions to engage in racial identity – Relevant behaviors. *Journal of Black Psychology, 36,* 226–250. doi:10.1177/0095798409344082

van Sertima, I. (1976). *They came before Columbus.* New York, NY: Random House

van Sertima, I. (1983). *Blacks in science: Ancient and modern.* New Brunswick, NJ: Transaction Publishers.

van Sertima, I. (1992). *Golden era of the moor.* New Brunswick, NJ: Transaction Publishers.

Walker, R. (2006). *When we ruled; The ancient and medieval history of Black civilizations.* London, England: Every Generation Media.

Wallace, D. L., & Bell, A. (1999). Being Black at a predominately White university. *College English, 61*(3), 307–327.

Walpole, M. (2008). Emerging from the pipeline: African American students, socioeconomic status, and college experiences and outcomes. *Research in Higher Education, 49*, 237–255. doi:10.1007/s11162-007-9079-y

Warde, B. (2008). Staying the course: Narratives of African American males who have completed a baccalaureate degree. *Journal of African American Studies, 12*, 59–72. doi:10.1007/s12111-007-9031-4

Watkins, W. H. (2001). *The White architects of Black education: Ideology and power in America, 1865–1954*. New York, NY: Teachers College Press.

Webber, T. L. (1978). *Deep like the rivers: Education in the slave quarter communities, 1831–1865*. New York, NY: W.W. Norton.

Wiggan, G. (2007). Race, school achievement and educational inequality: Towards a student-based inquiry perspective. *Review of Educational Research, 77*(3), 310–333.

Wiggan, G. (2008). From opposition to engagement: Lessons from high achieving African American students. *Urban Review, 40*(4), 317–349.

Wiggan, G. (2010). Afrocentricity and the Black intellectual tradition: Carter G. Woodson, W. E. B. Du Bois, and E. Franklin Frazier. *Journal of Pan African Studies, 3*(9), 128–151.

Wiggan, G. (2011). (Ed.). *Education for the new frontier: Race, education and triumph in Jim Crow America 1867–1945*. New York, NY: Nova Science Publishers.

Wiggan, G. (2015). *In search of a canon: European history and the imperialist state*. Rotterdam, The Netherlands: Sense Publishers-Springer.

Wiggan, G., Scott, L., Watson, M., & Reynolds, R. (2014). *Unshackled: Education for freedom, student achievement, and personal emancipation*. Rotterdam, The Netherlands: Sense Publishers-Springer.

Wilder, C. S. (2013). *Ebony and ivy: Race, slavery, and the troubled history of America's universities*. New York, NY: Bloomsbury Press.

Williams, E. (1966). *Capitalism and slavery*. New York, NY: Capricorn Books.

Williams, E. (1970). *From Columbus to Castro: The history of the Caribbean 1492–1969*. New York, NY: Vintage Books.

Wilson, W. J. (1980). *The declining significance of race: Blacks and changing American institutions*. Chicago, IL: University of Chicago Press.

Winston-Salem State University. (n.d.). *Stephen A. Smith*. Retrieved from https://winstonsalem.prestosports.com/about/hall_of_fame/Hall_of_Fame_Bios/ephen_A._Smith_Bio

Wood, J. (2002). House Negro versus field Negro: The inscribed image of race in television news representations of African-American identity. In R. R. Means-Coleman (Ed.), *Say it loud! African-American audiences, media, and identity* (pp. 95–113). New York, NY: Routledge.

Woodson, C. G. (1915). *The education of the Negro prior to 1861: A history of the education of the colored people from the United States from the beginning of slavery to the Civil War*. Kessinger Publishing. (Reprinted 2004)

Woodson, G. G. (1933). *The mis-education of the Negro*. Mineola, NY: Dover. (Reprinted 2005).

Yin, R. K. (2009). *Case study research: Design and methods*. Los Angeles, CA: Sage.

ABOUT THE AUTHORS

Greg Wiggan is an Associate Professor of Urban Education, Adjunct Associate Professor of Sociology, and Affiliate Faculty Member of Africana Studies at the University of North Carolina at Charlotte. His research addresses urban education and urban sociology in the context of school processes that promote high achievement among African American students and other underserved minority student populations. In doing so, his research also examines the broader connections between the history of urbanization, globalization processes and the internationalization of education in urban schools. His books include: *Global Issues in Education: Pedagogy, Policy, Practice, and the Minority Experience*; *Education in a Strange Land: Globalization, Urbanization, and Urban Schools – The Social and Educational Implications of the Geopolitical Economy*; *Curriculum Violence: America's new Civil Rights Issue*; *Education for the New Frontier: Race, Education and Triumph in Jim Crow America 1867–1945*; *Following the Northern Star: Caribbean Identities and Education in North American Schools; Unshackled: Education for Freedom, Student Achievement and Personal Emancipation*; and *In Search of a Canon: European History and the Imperialist State.*

Lakia Scott is an Assistant Professor in the Department of Curriculum and Instruction at Baylor University. Her research interests address urban education and student achievement.

INDEX

CPSIA information can be obtained at www.ICGtesting.com
Printed in the USA
BVOW06*1517141115

425301BV00003B/3/P

9 789463 003216